BLOODS AND CRIPS

THE AMERICAN MENACE

Michael Sims

Order this book online at www.trafford.com
or email orders@trafford.com

Most Trafford titles are also available at major online book retailers.

Printed in the United States of America.

ISBN: 978-1-4669-5515-8 (sc)
ISBN: 978-1-4669-5514-1 (hc)
ISBN: 978-1-4669-5516-5 (e)

Library of Congress Control Number: 2012915878

Trafford rev. 10/10/2012

 www.trafford.com

North America & international
toll-free: 1 888 232 4444 (USA & Canada)
phone: 250 383 6864 ♦ fax: 812 355 4082

Contents

Acknowledgment vii

Author's Notes xi

Prologue xv

Chapter 1: The Hardest Lil' Homeboy in the Hood 1

Chapter 2: A One Way Ticket to Captivity 38

Chapter 3: Consumed by the Most Vicious Beast 59

Chapter 4: Taming the Beast 82

Chapter 5: Cage within a Cage 106

Chapter 6: Setting Things Straight 135

Chapter 7: Fighting Amongst Ourselves to Fight for Ourselves 157

Appendix

Letters to my Holy Mom...179

Loving Thy Enemies...183

Final Comment...192

Acknowledgment

First and foremost, I acknowledge and praise God the Omniscient for blessing me with the mettle and physical abilities to endure my life's trials and tribulations.

My mother, Carrie Burton; evangelist for Christ. Thank you for staying by my side unfaltering for all of my life, I love you ineffable.

My cousins, Linda and Kenneth, thank you for your constant help in bringing this memoir to past, I love you much.

Mr. Fred (Magic) Price and G-Winn, thank you for your constant support and believing in this project in the earliest stages of my endeavor.

Mr. M'Fupa M'tu, thank you for the inspiration and encouragement to compose memoir.

Mr. Steve Harvey, comedian, radio host of "100.3 The Beat." Thank you for the love and support you have shown for the unfortunate brothers and sisters of all ethnicities who are enthralled behind these prison walls. Your morning shout-outs on the radio show to prisoners are very uplifting and inspiring. And thank you for the "Hoodie Awards." This award should be a national celebration to the urban communities, especially the celebrities who are products of the 'Hoods—without the 'Hood support they'd still be in the 'Hood.

Mr. Master-P., CEO of No Limit Records, rap artist, entrepreneur. Thank you for maintaining your authenticity to the urban community. It is an infusion of hope for such wretched brothers to strive despite the diabolical confusions that stand to deter our ambitious desires to soar beyond the concrete graves of our infernal conditions.

Mrs. Sista Soul, radio host of KHSU, activist for prisoners' human rights, and devoted egalitarian for all. Thank you for your adamant, vigorous support in our crusade. It is very much needed and appreciated immensely. During the month of December 2009 you were unexpectedly stripped from the airwaves of the Pelican Bay State Prison broadcasting system that no longer allow us the euphonious sounds of your oldies. It is like depriving prisoners of rehabilitation of the encouraging programs and words of productivity that you had provided us.

Mr. Jeff Johnson, BET personality, community activist. Thank you for your support. You are the spearhead and grassroots inspiration to the political minded gang society brother such as me who yearn to transform lawless individuals into law abiding people for the good of our communities. The lobbyist that you launched for the suffrage of former prisoners is something worth pursuing. Furthermore, prisoners should have the human rights to vote for those public officials who have the humane desire to help correct our virulent conditions in prison as well as our communities across the nation.

Mr. Ving Rhames, actor, community activist and a frontline proponent for the reconciliation of the gangs in Los Angeles, California. Thank you for your support in this area in which many have forsaken.

Mr. Birdman, rap artist, CEO Cash Money-Young Money Records, and W.C., rap artist, I extend homage to you brothers for representing yourselves (publicly) in a dignified manner. For there are far too many caricatures claiming to represent our communities.

Mr. Baron Davis, NBA Clippers, product of our community in Los Angeles, California. Thank you for shining light on our continuous urban blight. The documentary "Bloods and Crips: Made in America" on the "PBS Broadcasting" was uplifting for many to continue to be the healing voice against gang violence.

Baby Laniak (LA DLB) and Young Smokey (SDB), thank you for giving me the constructive criticism that prompted me to dilate further on my youth in this memoir.

Author's Notes

I would like for those who may have an objective opinion of the language that I use to narrate my life, by which we live, to understand that I could have very well written this book without offensive language. But to do so would have altered the true nature of our social conditions, languages, and attitudes.

My primary objective is to reach out to the most wretched brothers and sisters in the nation. Many people may naively believe that people in the urban communities doesn't read books, especially gang members. I intend to refute that denigrating stigma to some degree, for I am an exemplary. I cannot speak (too) much (for) our common people in Urban Society. But, I do know that being inquisitive is intrinsic to human nature.

I am an expert in gangs and law-enforcement. For I've been profoundly entwined with the two for over thirty-six years. The most hardened gang members in society I doubt would actually read a book, although educated enough to do so.

Perhaps a book cover such as this would indubitably attract their attentions, due to it being a direct relation to their life. And may browse through it sporadically. On the contrary, the million or more gang members who are incarcerated across the nation, the vast majority are avid readers. Especially when the subject is that of enthralled. Sad, but true facts, confinement is where many of us educate ourselves. For desirous motive to correspond with family, friends, and relations with society in general. There have been literally over fifty gang members and prison officials who read this manuscript. And in some way they were all unanimous in saying they were affected in a positive way, by the message I am promoting to the gang members.

My unvarnished truth, attitude, and belief system is what they can relate to as I did when I was young and a ruffian. When I displayed the book-cover to them, without hesitation the utterance of "let me read that book" flowed from their mouths.

The most promising comment that inspired me to believe that my life experience would help many hardened gang members realize that we are a serious problem to our communities, was the inspiring words made by a new found Crip friend, Quas from "Palmer Bloc" (Compton Crips.) twenty-eight-year-old Quas wrote, "Yeah, Ridah Mike, I read the whole manuscript in two days.

It was a page turner, and an easy read. But when I first started reading it, I was like this is just another one of those gang books. When I got to the last two chapters, it had an unexpected turn that I didn't see coming."

"It totally caught me off guard! The things that you wrote about (self-destruction) I'd heard so many times before. But the way you explained it, I felt the connections and it made me reflect back to all of the wrong I did to contribute to the condition that we are in. I've read many autobiographies before, but by far this is the best one I've ever read, hands down! There aren't too many hub-and-dubs (Compton-Watts) Original Gangsta homies who I have respect for, but now you are one of those who I respect and will support!" And another young twenty-four-year-old Crip friend of mines, named Puncho from Nutty Bloc' (Compton Crip), was so excited when he returned the manuscript he blurted, "Man, this book cans easily sale well over a million copies. Me and my cellie enjoyed it!" I'm not an expert in the publishing business by any means. But to be honest, when I initially set out to write my memoir it was compelled by the effusive rage that dwelled within me to promulgate to the masses of young Bloods in the California prison system why I was the most abhorrent and dired Blood member in my era. Being the first generation of Bloods and Crips to enter the prison system.

Thus, there has been many years of aspersions propagated against me by the first generation. Furthermore, when the prison officials saw the book-cover they immediately confiscated it and handed it over to the Institutional Gang Investigating Unit (IGI). A prison bureau who's primarily designed to investigate all gang activities in the prison.

I contacted my facility Lieutenant Johnson to ask him to look into the matter for me, and he assured me that he would. He asked me, "What's the name of it?" I said, "Bloods and Crips: The American Menace!" Lieutenant Johnson burst into sudden deep resonating laughter. Then with a grin he said, "I'm sure you won't get an argument out of that one!" I assumed our conversation was coincidental, because he told me that there were rumors that the Bloods and Crips were plotting to hit the staff. And he asked me what I knew about it. I said, "This is the first time hearing about this from you." He said, "I think you know something!"

He was aggressive as though he expected me to tell, had I known something, I said, "Lieutenant Johnson, I don't know anything about that, and if I did I wouldn't tell you. I'm not a rat! And I don't think it's true, because one of your sources probably would have told you." I was honest, and he realized I was being straight forward with him.

Two weeks later he called me back to his office to enlighten me that he had spoken to (IGI) Institutional Gang Investigating Lieutenant Gentry, and he said he perused the entire manuscript and didn't see anywhere that I violated prison policy of manuscript writing, and he would return it.

In Lieutenant Johnson's ordinance miens he exclaimed, "They said it was some good writing, I'm-a hafta go and get me a copy!" My escorting unit officer, Ybarra-a.k.a.-Red said, "No Lieutenant, you got to go and buy it like everyone else." He gave the Lieutenant a friendly reprimand. My sincere desire, is to give these young dudes the incentive to think before senselessly killing people, and consider being a positive solution to our oppressed conditions. I will then be content with my contributions of helping ameliorate the gang society by undoing the vileness that I have partaken with the first generation. Many of the first rooted Bloods and Crips who've helped create this horrible condition, have repudiated the 'B' (Bloods) and 'C' (Crips) to let the young homies 'hood condition deteriorate by the years. The words of Former Bloods and Crips who are now community activists doesn't convey weight with most hardened gang members, which is the core group that needs to be reached.

Prologue

When a person that hails from the criminal underworld turns into an author, he is inevitably named a sell-out at best and a snitch at worse. He is often accused of exposing the cause and jeopardizing its further advancements. Kody "Monster Kody" Scott is a prime example.

It wasn't until 2002 that I had the opportunity to read his autobiography *Monster*. For year I had been curious as to its contents, for the vast majority of gang members had dubbed him a "snitch" for his efforts at shining light on the gang culture. The infamous 8-tray Gangsta Crip, Lil' Football (who was caught on camera hitting the truck driver Reginald Denny in the head with a brick in the 1992 Los Angeles rebellion), wasn't too fond of Monster's blabbering mouth and punched him in it, knocking out one of his teeth.

He's currently here in Pelican Bay State Prison General Population (GP). My opinion of Monster is that he's a very intelligent brother who made good out of his troubled lifestyle, but he mentioned some incidents that gave his adversaries valid reason to speak derogatory about him, being that there is no statute of limitation for murder offenses. I wish not to label him a snitch though he is not the maven he proclaimed to be in the gang society.

If so, he would have been would have been very discreet in his event writing. Having said that, it is my intention to avoid such a vicious trap. All of the events that I write about are real, although some names have been changed in order to remain true to form and protect the guilty. Some incidents I had to be vague on, while others I had to completely avoid. I did not write about anything that could get a man arrested, sent to the hole, or divorced.

I am well respected and infamous Blood throughout this State of California prison system. I will not compromise one principle under any circumstances.

Every detail that I give is documented facts and I am not exposing anything that is not already on file. I merely promulgate, what is in the dictum of the homie, Cabbage Peanut's, from (Cabbage Patch Piru) "Public-Information." I am very guarded as to what I say, for there are malicious haters in here who will read my every word, for the sole intention of finding an opportunity to obliterate my character (as they have attempted to discredit me for the last twenty-seven years). For there are many charlatans whose true identities have been deceitfully concealed by their so-called loved ones.

Of course there are many jealous brothers who are going to hate and gossip like high school girls. No matter what you do in life, you create enemies rather your deeds are good or bad. Martin Luther King Jr. is my best exemplary of our times. All he did was dedicated his life to being a minister, philanthropist, and community activist—and he were despised by millions for doing so.

Therefore, as long as I remain true to myself and the Blood struggle, a freedom fighter. I am content with myself and all of the positive contributions I've made for the Blood's society and the race. This book is not meant to glamorize violence in our communities.

In fact, the intent is the opposite. I have not spoken about the shootings and perhaps murders I've associated myself with in my youth. I'm not proud of the life I lived, but I am very proud of the fact that I changed my life and evolved into a man of principle and a righteous functioning human being. There is not sense of honor in the senseless killings of innocent people, especially against oppressed people who have been suffering all of their lives. I hope this book can be a catalyst and inspire the young and older brothers to fight for a cause worth living and dying for. I am one of you. I'm the epitome of your destructive lifestyle.

We who commit senseless crimes are the sole justification for the government's need to design such biased laws as three strikes, crack cocaine versus powder cocaine, and the many other laws that inundate us in these prisons.

Nevertheless, its brothers like NFL's great, Jim Brown who genuinely cares about us and continues to open his home to us. He makes this struggle worthwhile.

So, I encourage all brothers to support brothers like Jim Brown, Steve Harvey, Jeff Johnson, and the many others of their stature. Bloods, Crips, Thugs, or whatever title you might hold—to support brothers such as mentioned to help ourselves.

I strongly believe they hold our best interest at heart. I've been a Blood member of the Nine-Duce (92nd Street) Bishops for thirty-seven years. And twenty-nine of those years, and still counting—have been spent in prison, boldly representing Bloodism. In all of my prison years, I've had the privilege and misfortune of meeting a lot of Bloods: some being soldiers, scholars, authentic, phonies, cowards, and stealthy agents who would falsely bring a brother to ruins for the good of the prison officials.

There have been a lot of negative rumors about my character. Some dastard have labeled me a trouble-maker, simply because of the strength and genuine love I have for the struggle, which has been a major part of my survival for more than thirty-seven years.

The true soldiers who took the opportunity to know and judge me by my actions, now know that the hating individuals, who spoke of me in slanderous terms were doing nothing but misguiding them with lies. In order for us to stop the negativity amongst ourselves, we must learn to focus on our real plights. For those individuals who claim to be Bloods and Crips for life, there are a hundred or more Bloods and Crips on death-row. What are we doing to stop the racist and unfair judicial system from unjustly murdering our comrades? I have a comrade on death-row. His name is Big Time Sadiki. He has been on death-row for a little over twenty-six years for a crime he didn't commit. But what are the so-called homies who are free doing to save him? Nothing. Yet, they are financially capable of contributing to his liberty.

As Bloods and Crips, we can be a positive force to be reckoned with. It is a known fact that we are the people's army. But it is also a known fact that we are condemned because we have been a dysfunctional, and in most cases, a self-destructive force.

For example, take the beating of the motorist Rodney King, by the possible white supremacists with police badges. If it weren't for our rebellious protesting, the police officers would have gotten away with giving King a publicized ass kicking. Because of our efforts, as urban soldiers, the courts must enforce the laws that prohibit such blatant brutality.

That's why it is our responsibilities to fight for ourselves. We cannot sit around waiting for the tokens or bourgeois black society to do for us. They view us as being the problem that plagues our race.

If we're honest with ourselves, then we are part of the problem. But if someone isn't helping us rectify our conditions, and constantly tossing negative criticism, then they need to simply learn how to keep their poisonous mouth shut!

On the other hand, if they are supporting our communities such as Magic Johnson does, then we should give them our support fully. I love and respect what Oprah Winfrey does for all people, as far as her philanthropy is concerned.

She conveys it well and is an exemplary for the world. Many hardened gang members respected her. But I love the candid and sincere words Magic uttered to her during their interview on her show. "But little Africa is right here, America!" he exclaimed.

Referring to the lofty deed she did by providing the young sisters in South Africa the multimillion dollar school. The benefactor was immaculate, but Magic was absolutely right. We must first build ourselves here as a people, and then we will have political and economic power to help Africa and the many other oppressed countries around the world.

We have to respect sisters like Congresswoman Maxine Waters and brothers like Reverend Al Sharpton and the many others who have proven to be our true community leaders. We can be a power and positive force collectively.

We should be indignant towards those in our communities who come to prison for the senseless killings of our children, senior citizens, and innocent people. Yet, instead we sit around and share coffee and conversation with them, only affected when these heinous crimes happen to our immediate families and friends. Additionally, we shouldn't forget about the so-called "Gansta Rappers" in our society. They are nothing but perpetrators capitalizing on our youths hunger for guidance. They are simply misguiding our youths with bull-shit. Most of those brothers are only taking advantage of the people's pain and suffering.

For instance, when the rap star Notorious Big was killed, there was a discussion on Black Entertainment Television (BET) hosted by Tavis Smiley, who is a brilliant voice for our communities. One of his guests on the show was Willie Dee of the rap group "The Ghetto Boys." He made an astonishing statement while on national television. I was flabbergasted when he stated, "I know what I am about to say is going to be very unpopular. But, if I had seen who killed Biggie, I would be giving a statement right now!" At the same time, this dude was putting out rap songs encouraging our youths to kill-up the whole house.

One verse I vividly remember, "You cried when yo' grand momma died, now you finna go see her!" this is a vicious, vicious game that these dudes are playing with our youths lives. To influence gullible minds to violate the law in such hideous ways, and then turn around and turn them over to the authorities I believe to be equivalent to the 1800s Negroes turning over other free blacks to the slave master's for material benefits or other dastardly motives. I really liked listening to "The Ghetto Boys." But I will never buy a tape or CD with that busta rapping on it. We can continue to be a menace to our communities and ourselves, or we can be revolutionaries against those who impose oppression and injustice upon us. I'm not advocating hatred against any person or ethnic group. For Bloods and Crips have never been racially motivated, our 'homeboys' are that of all ethnicities.

It's about fighting injustice, no matter who inflicts it against us. It appears to me that our own race can be more destructive towards each other than the Ku Klux Klan. When the adversary looks and acts like you, it's a hell of a disguise, and disadvantage. Before you realize who the enemy is, the results could be the same as the ones that brought an end to our "Black Panther Party."

White supremacists or outside forces never had an opportunity to ruin the Panthers. They ruined themselves when they lost sight of their original goals and objectives.

One elderly homie (Dadisi, a.k.a. Alias Lo, West-side Piru, co-founder of the Compton Piru-Bloods) told me that the U.S. Government led by J. Edgar Hoover, (former 1924-1972 director of the Federal Bureau of Investigation) abolished the Panthers. During this sad hateful period of blatant racial discrimination in America, it was Hoover behooving duties to bring an end to the Panthers. Of course it wasn't morally right. But still, I defend my belief that the Panthers destroyed themselves by permitting their surroundings to become unstable and infiltrated. Their obligation was to have the Panthers so tightly together it would have been nearly impossible for the espionages to permeate the organization. We have to stop blaming other people for our debacles.

Our present conditions are much more facilitated than the Panthers era. All we have to do is build ourselves legally. So the bottom line is we have to help ourselves and stay true to our objective. Only the means can justify the end.

When I first entered the prison system (San Quentin) at twenty-one years old, it was like a training camp against oppression. It stood for raising cultural awareness in brothers. Now it's a gang of wayward dastards who are working with the oppressors, running around the prison system with pimp and gangstamentality. When in reality, the administration is gangstering them out of their dignity and treating them like the "Bitches" they are trying to marginalize.

For those of you who don't hear the cry and urgent need for us to consolidate our forces, so that we can begin working towards the reunification and reparation of our true selves and subsistence, then your mind set is equivalent to those who are racist. You are an enemy to yourself and those of your race. And should be corrected by the inevitable power of righteousness.

Chapter 1

The Hardest Lil' Homeboy
in the Hood

I was born November 15, 1960, in the state of Louisiana. At the age of three, my mother came to California and we lived in the city of Watts. She brought along with her my oldest brother, Earl, my oldest sister, Patricia, my younger sister, Elizabeth, and my first cousin, Verna who I love dearly and equally to my siblings.

We were the typical, struggling, poor black family living in America's urban community. I recall my mother doing everything she could possibly do to help us. We were a close family who didn't have much, and lived on welfare like most poor families in the 'hood.

When we first arrived in California, we lived in a church in Watts for about two weeks, and then we moved into a house a few houses away from the church.

Two years after being in California, my mother gave unwedded birth to a third sister. My mother named her Jacqueline. Now it was six kids she had to tend to. A year later, she met and married my stepfather, with whom she had two more children. My younger brother, Ruben, and my youngest sister, Dorine.

Now there were eight kids in the family. Having a father in the home made life easier because now there was someone to provide for the family.

All of my life I can remember my mother being very religious. God came before everything and everyone, including her kids and husband. We had to attend church every Sunday. It was mandatory. I hated going to church. It was boring. I did everything possible—any crafty trick to avoid going. Occasionally, I would succeed, but most of the time it was to no avail. I believe that my mother was, and is a religious fanatic. Currently at three years old she takes portions of her government dole to rent buildings in the neighborhood to do God's will, as she would say—to hold church services. I truly respect her dedication, but I feel she's too excessive in her crusade. I love her so much that I'd rather see her owning her own church more so than me getting out of prison. And hating this prison lifestyle is an understatement for me.

My mother and stepfather whipped my siblings and me harshly, especially me. They used switches, belts, extension cords, and once I recall getting scourged with a water hose by my stepfather.

To be honest, in retrospect our whippings were for justifiable reasons. But much too harsh, the slightest misconduct would result in a painful beating.

I now believe that this fallacious whipping method that our parents used to discipline us was a curse indoctrinated by thralldom to keep human beings under complete control. I believe that this is why our neighborhoods are so violent. We inherit this fallacy to believe that violence is the source of dealing with all problems.

My stepfather was a big man, around 6'4" and 280 pounds. I believe he was a coward also. When I was around five or six years old, I vividly remember seeing an indelible incident involving him.

There was I, a very young lad sitting in the back seat of the car. As he began to park the car in front of the apartments, I observed him having parking complications with another man who was also parking in the front. He got out the car, as he and the other man accosted each other, I saw the man hit my stepfather in the mouth and my stepfather walked away.

I assume he didn't see any logic in violence at his expense. I ironically, perhaps two years after witnessing him falter in that troubling situation he made me fight a neighboring boy named Fred, who was bigger than me. He used to somewhat bully me, but after the fight I wasn't afraid of him anymore. I kind of felt that my stepfather was proud of me for doing well for my seven-year-old self. But the whippings kept coming.

Around two years after he encouraged me to fight Fred, my mother decided to question him about whipping us so harshly. He became so enraged that he hit her.

I didn't see him hit her, but I surely saw my mother crying. He utilized that incident as a motive to abandon the family like the dastard he was. He moved out of the house leaving my mother to take care of eight children by herself. But she continued to raise us to the best of her ability, and vigorously instilled Christian values into us. We were Baptist at the time.

Most black folks in America have adopted Christianity as their religion, which is fine, but the Bible has been altered many times throughout its history, and still today it continues to be revised to some extent or another. Nevertheless, the religious belief that she instilled in us assured me indubitably that God exists.

But as one becomes mature, wiser, and examines the world and life experiences for themselves they can draw their own conclusions about religion. I come to the conclusion that agnosticism is the best approach for me. I believe that no one knows the true existence of God, everyone has their own theory. And in my observation all religions are embroiled in a power struggle against each other, just like the political parties. Religious people can deceive, scare, and confuse billions of people throughout the world. Such as, if a person doesn't worship God in this or that manner, they will perish and suffer in this or that manner. Personally, I am content with just believing in the creator, God. And being the best person that I can possibly be. During my entire youth, my mother told me God will see us through. When matters got worse, we would rely on prayer. At age eleven, I recall being very angry when I blurted to my mother, "If there's a God, why are we so poor?" "Don't worry about material things, you can't take them to Heaven with you," she replied. This concept was disturbing to my young mind. I wanted some heaven while I was still on earth.

When we arrived in Watts in 1963, the most infamous gangs in the nation, Bloods and Crips had not come into existence yet. But, the first school I attended was Ridder Elementary. The only clear recollection I have is starting the third grade. Perhaps it is because of the brutal teacher, Mrs. Heart, who didn't have much of a heart at all. I remember one day she gave the class a test. I thought I was being sly when I asked the girl sitting next to me to let me cheat off her papers. Mrs. Heart heard me, and pinched me so hard it literally burst the skin on my arm to the point where it bled. I didn't tell my mother out of fear of getting punished for trying to cheat. Well, she taught me a lesson there with her unprofessional tactics. I never tried to cheat again in her class.

I graduated to the fourth grade. My teacher there was Mrs. Arnold. She also punched me to the bleeding point. She became so frustrated with me because I wasn't an apted kid. I remember how she used to try and teach me to read and spell. Then she would have a group session where we would have to read portions of a book to the class. I hated those sessions. My reading was extremely terrible. I tried my best to learn and enjoyed trying to be smart, but it was very difficult to grasp things that were being told to me. I didn't know the word or the diagnosis for my abnormal learning ability, but now I believe it was dyslexia, and still today it's difficult for me to learn. But I am determined when I devote myself to whatever curricular that I undertake.

At age ten, my family moved to another neighborhood, but still we resided in Watts. In this new district I would enroll in Graham Elementary. I was now in fifth grade. I flunked twice, remaining in fifth and sixth grade for two years each.

In Graham, Gregory Popular was the undisputed "king of the school." It is what we termed a person that could beat up everyone, and Harvis was runner up. They were both in the sixth grade. I'd known Gregory before moving to this new neighborhood because he lived down the street from my Aunt Lillie-B.

Therefore, I met him and his family when I would visit my aunt's house. On a couple of occasions we squared off on the streets during my visits, but basically it was a kiddy aloof type of fight. I didn't think I could whip him, though I was the one who fomented the dispute as a tactical means of trying to intimidate him. but he was rigid. I liked him, he wasn't a bully. He could just whip everyone, but could also respect everyone as well.

One day at recess while playing basketball, I got into an argument with Harvis. We squared off. The teachers came and broke it up.

Harvis walked away and I hit him in the back of his head real hard and he started crying. The teachers took us to the principal's office. The principal lectured us and sent us about our way. Harvis put word out around the school that he was after me. That term was a serious threat at this young and gullible age.

After school I went home. I was a bit nervous, but later that day I went to the street that he lived on to see if I could see him on the block. He lived on "Bandera," which was the headquarters (street) for the gang members. He never came out-side. The next day at school he didn't confront me so that was the end of our problem. A few months after that Gregory Popular and Harvis graduated to junior high school.

But now there was Gregory Brooks and a tomboy named Shubby who was waiting in line to obtain this prestigious title of being "King of the School." I was told they had already fought before I enrolled. Their bout was said to have been a draw. I never cared about being the king of anything. I just always felt a desire to punk the dudes who thought they were hard. Shubby and I squared off at recess. I popped her in her eye a couple of times with quick flicks of the back of my fingers, and that was the end of our desire to compete with each other. We became amiable, which was preferable by me anyway. I didn't see any dignity in fighting a girl, but she urged me on. One evening after school, while playing basketball on the schoolyard, I saw an opportunity to instigate a fight with Gregory. I said, "You think you are king of the school, huh?"

"I am," he replied.

"Well, let's fight." I responded to his claim.

We squared off into our fighting stances. He wasn't as aggressive as I anticipated he would be. We threw a few punches and he started backing up, which emboldened me. I then backed him up literally from the basketball court to the corner of his block where he lived, which perhaps was a half-a-mile away. A few kids were observing the fight, but it was so boring they all went home.

Except Anthony, who by appearance looked much harder than me.

Anthony was a bulgy-fat, but robust in form, dark-skinned, with a harsh demeanor. This guy decided that it was his duty to protect Brooks, so he took Brook's place and started fighting me. Brooks saw an opportunity to ease away from the scene, leaving Anthony and me alone.

Anthony did me the same way that I had done Brooks. He backed me up all the way to my house that was about a mile from our starting point. We went through alleys and all that was necessary just to prove a foolish point.

But I was winning the fight despite my backward notions. Because I was hitting him at will, with my back-hand flick. He never hit me during the whole fight. I played antics with him, knowing that I had exposed the debunkness of his persona. I would say to him as I pointed to his legs or other parts of his person.

"You got a bug on your leg."

He would look and I'd pop him somewhere on his face. And this idiot looked as I duped him several times. The flicks weren't much of a force, but they wore him down and into frustration.

Finally, I got tired of popping him. I ran over to my mother's car to get a bumper jack. I came back and hit him on his leg with it. I didn't try to hurt him, my deception was to make him think I was nuts. And it worked. He went home and I went into my house. I'm sure he thought he really chose the wrong fight after those horrific results.

Because the following morning on our way to school, he was submissive as one could be. From that moment, until I came to prison, I marginalized him severely almost every time I saw him in our 'hood. I would literally kick him in his ass and take his money.

My first arrest, I was a few months from turning eleven years old. While lounging around after school, a couple of kids and I decided to break into Graham's cafeteria to steal some ice cream and cookies. We broke the window and went inside and started eating and stuffing food in our pockets. The other kids had enough sense to get in and out quickly. I stayed a bit longer than everyone else. Unfortunately for me I got caught by the police inside the cafeteria. They handcuffed me and escorted me to the police car, and off to jail I went. There I was ten years old in Firestone police department for the very first time.

When I entered the jail I was scoffed by a Mexican policeman. He pushed me violently against the wall, and then slapped me twice in the face. I was very apprehensive and didn't know what to expect. He escorted me to the back area of the jail where the offices desks were located.

As he ordered me to sit at the desk, I didn't know what to think of his behavior. He said to me, "You have two choices. The first one is to be booked for juvenile hall; the second is to write some standards." I didn't say anything, but clearly I chose the second with bodily gestures. He set a pencil and paper in front of me on the desk and ordered me to write, "I am a thief," a hundred times.

I gazed at him in fear and total ignorance that indicated, "I can't spell, and I am a thief." And I didn't have the courage to tell him I couldn't spell it. But his instincts figured it out and he wrote down the first line for me.

I completed the standards in perhaps an hour or so. He then sent me home to my mother whom he had called to notify of my burglary. She was waiting for me to whip me as usual when I had gotten into trouble. After writing those refraining words, I continued to steal, and my mother would blurt out in rage when I got arrested, "You are going to spend the rest of your life in prison."

I knew she had always wanted the best for me, but when your words are tactless towards people, especially kids, they can be more destructive than constructive.

Still to this very day I don't know if the policeman's method of punishment was meant to deter my criminal behavior or to infuse the notion that I am a thief. I wonder if he would have made his own progeny write such standards had they been a young delinquent as I once was.

Around this period of time my gang was starting to formalize. I noticed older guys having meetings on Fridays on my schoolyard after school. I would go to the meetings at eleven years old and sit quietly and listen to the leader who started Bishops. He was Bobby Lavador. A short guy maybe 5'7" and 180 pounds. He was a Kung fu expert, black belt was his degree. I'd heard, since I've been incarcerated that he died of a heart attack.

I observed Clady Clay as being the most feared Bishop during that time. And Randy Turpin was the most beloved, and the leader of my immediate set. First we were Baby Bishops, then a year later we altered our name to Block Bishops.

We came into existence in 1971, and shortly thereafter we would become part of the synthesis of other Los Angeles gangs, known today as Bloods.

I was the first youngest active member of the Bishops. I had influence over all the kids in my age bracket. But I mostly hung out with the older gang members.

The first stage of gang activity I participated in as a Baby Bishop I recall, Randy, and a group of Baby Bishops and I patrolling our neighborhood looking for Crips walking through our territory. We would catch them and beat them down. I once recall all of us deciding to travel and venture into the Crips' neighborhood to battle with them—being that one day we got frustrated that we couldn't find any pedestrian Crips coming through our neighborhood.

Around 9 P.M. Randy, me, and five other older Bishops walked down Firestone Boulevard into their turf. When we reached Charles Drew Jr. High School we turned around to go back. I assumed Randy didn't want to go to deep into their territory by means of walking. On our way back we went through the back-streets of their houses to see if they would be hanging out in their 'hood. There were about seven of them standing on the sidewalk in front of a house. Randy said, "Ooo-wee!" "We finna walk through a pack of them." The count was even. We made it to them, and the only thing that kept us from brawling was everyone knew each of them in a decent type of way. Archie and Dirt-Bomb, who were brothers, and factors in their 'hood respected Randy, and he respected them. They embraced, talked for a few minutes and we proceeded our walk home.

I was relieved, and grateful that a turned out as it did. Being the youngest at eleven, and everyone else sixteen and older, I surely would have gotten my young ass kicked or killed. But the chances of being killed in this era wasn't that great. During this time the gangs didn't have the type of guns that the present gangs have today.

I remember in 1971, in a 92nd Street alley, we had a meeting and were preparing to conduct a mass shooting of Crips. there were approximately sixty members who attended the meeting. Bobby loudly asked, "Who all got guns?" out of the sixty Bishops, only three members raised their hands. Bobby then said, "All right, we're gonna raid a gun store." In broad daylight on a Saturday morning around 11 A.M., he told us to meet up in the back alley of the gun store, which was stationed on the busy street, of Firestone Boulevard.

Not many of us had cars. We had to walk though the Crip's neighborhood to reach the gun store. We made our way by walking in groups of two's, five's, or six's, and riding in a few cars. Coincidently, the Crips were having their meeting at Charles Drew Jr. High School on the football field. My homeboy, Randy, started beating down Crips and taking their leather jackets on our way to the store. Crips started whistling. They had a distinguishing whistle to alarm other Crips of danger in their neighborhood. All who heard it would come and aid the Crips. because of this, and the police patrol cars that were starting to appear, we had to retreat.

To make it back to our neighborhood about ten of my homeboys and I had to run through their meeting. I could make it through them. There were easily a hundred of them. I was in tangible grounds, but I quickly started climbing a fence that was very high, perhaps fifty-feet. This big light complexioned Crip said to me, "Get down you little nigga!" he attempted to grab me, but I avoided his maneuver and made it over the fence and back to my neighborhood, unscathed.

My homeboys, Randy and Cecil came back with knots all on their faces. "One Crip had a gun. He pulled the trigger but it didn't fire, so he started beating me with the gun!" said Randy. Other than Randy and Cecil's minor injuries, we all made it back safely to the neighborhood. We laughed and talked abut that experience.

Shortly after this incident, I established a solid reputation in my neighborhood. By now I had finally graduated from Graham, and enrolled in Charles Drew Junior High School, located within the Crips' neighborhood. One afternoon word was pervasive amongst all of my homeboys. After school, the Crips would be looking to beat down on all Bishops they saw.

My homeboys were in a state of panic. After school, they came home to avoid the confrontation with the Crips. needless to say, I was afraid too.

My homeboy Tyde and I were walking with three females that lived in our neighborhood. I had a crush on one, her name was Gayle. Nine Crips accosted us. I wasn't about to display cowardice behavior in front of Gayle.I wasn't going to run, though I wanted to. During this early gang stage, this particular Crip set was called Neighborhood Crips.

Their leader, Carry Gate-Mouth knew me. He recognized me and said, "That cat-eyed nigga is a Bishop!" he had a pipe in his hand. The Crips saw Tyde but didn't know he was a Bishop. Neither did he makes any indication to let them know he was one.

Tyde calmly said to Carry Gate-Mouth, "Put the pipe down and fight him one-on-one." By then I had picked up a stick. Tyde eased the pipe out of Carry's hand. I put the stick down. We started fighting, throwing several blows, but I got the best of him.

I busted his lip and then he grabbed me. Now the fight became a wrestling match and he had me in a headlock. It felt as though he was pulling my hair. Sarcastically I remarked, "Look at this nigga pulling my hair like a little bitch!"

The observers laughed, even his homeboys Tyde and the Crips pulled us apart. The Crips went their way. Tyde, the girls, and I continued to walk home.

Later that day, word had circulated through my neighborhood and had reached my older homeboys. They were all proud of me because of the way I represented Bishops. Not knowing that Gayle was my biggest inspiration. Word was, "Mike Sims was the only Bishop who stayed and fought." They all embraced me as being the hardest lil' homeboy in the 'hood.

Three years had passed by. In 1976, at a neighborhood disco club, the leader of my set, Randy noticed that a couple of new young Bishops named Rosco and Fish had come to the neighborhood to take a leadership position. Randy suggested that I take such a role.

All of the original homies had gotten older and had somewhat retired from gang activities. At sixteen, I was much more involved in stealing and robbing people (strong-arm robberies). Occasionally, I would gangbang when it was necessary. I continued to function as a juvenile delinquent, doing everything my mother despised. And now I also despise the trouble and distress I caused people in my youth. Often I imagined the pain I would feel if my mother was duped, or victimized by some young or old ruffian. My mother did everything she could to raise me right. And I turned out to be very troubled. The lil' homie Ray J'smother said it best for all of the good law-abiding moms in our urban communities,

"You can't write a book on raising kids!" she exclaimed.

My first arrest was at ten years old for burglary. I was released many times for burglary, robbery, and snatching purses before I became a ward of the county. On June 7, 1974, I was placed in Everette's Boys' Home. By this time the Bloods and Crips had become prominent throughout Los Angeles county.

Crips came into existence in 1969, founded by Raymond Washington and Ronnie Bam being amongst Raymond's first five Crips. the Bloods emerged shortly after the Crips, as far as synthesizing the non-Crip gangs and accepting the term Bloods is concerned. Being that the Crips hit the scene first, their initiations far exceeded the Bloods. They outnumbered us perhaps ten-to-one. Thirty-seven years later, we have lessened this hiatus to maybe four-to-one, and I believe to be equal in count, nationwide. The first incident I encountered in the boys' home was with a Crip named Nec' Bone from Harlem 30's.

He accused me of cheating him in a game of pool. I believe it was a means of testing my courage. Hence, I accepted his challenge. My ability to fight was often underestimated, but I whipped his ass in he recreation room.

He couldn't accept defeat. So the next day we fought again in the backyard and that one was a draw. He conceded and we became amicable. The Crips commonly jumped Bloods, but occasionally when chivalrous Crips recognized a valorous Blood, he would respect him and permit his homeboys to combat with a Blood one-on-one. A lot of Crips didn't like the one-on-one battles. The Bloods had the advantage. The home was located in the middle of a Blood's neighborhood. The Ross Snyder's Park Pirus—today known as 30's – 40's Pirus.

They would catch the Crips at the park across the street from the home, or down the street at the store. The Bloods would beat them down and send them back to the boys' home with their faces busted-up. I recall, the Bloods, once coming over to the home trying to provoke the Crips to come outside to fight them. But their endeavor was to no avail. There were three of us in this boys' home and thirteen Crips. The three of us were in a vulnerable position. The Bloods who wielded the neighborhood had created a very hostile gangbanging atmosphere with the Crips that we had to live with. However, we remained firm. One night around 11:30 P.M. everyone was sound asleep. Nec' Bone and I decided to play mischievous games with the other wards. While they slept in their beds, we put matches between their toes and lit them to see what kind of shocking reactions we would get from them.

It was hilarious to see them fools jump out of their sleep in a state of panic. I wasn't expecting these dudes to run to the counselor and tell on us, but they did.

The home had a mediating program to solve the problems amongst the wards. We would all form a meeting in the recreation room and vote on which disciplinary actions were suitable for the infraction. We used a consensus voting system. Being that I had two fights prior to this incident, the other wards had two options of disciplinary actions that they could impose upon me. The first was to send me back to the juvenile hall that I had just come from, East Lake Central located in downtown Los Angeles. The second choice was to send me to a new boys' home.

Which they thought was much more lenient than sending me back to the hall. In September1974, I was placed in West Marlin Boys' Home. I knew every time I went to a different environment, I had to bust-up somebody in order to set an example that I was no punk-Blood. This home was located in the Harlem 30's Crips' neighborhood. There were thirteen Crips in this home, and I made the third Blood in this home. One Blood was Jasper from Pueblo Bishops. So, we had connections both being Bishops, but this dude was an absolute coward. He was kissing the Crips' asses so they wouldn't kick his ass. They manipulated this fool into fighting me. The other Blood was Larry. He was a Brim. The Crips used to run him out of the home every weekend, as though it was a planned recreation. The head counselor was Mr. Woods. He was perhaps around his mid or early 40's.

He was about 5'7" and 180 pounds. It appeared Mr. Woods could have been Black and Indian judging by his physical appearance. He had naturally straight wavy, black hair, sprinkled with gray, and a smooth dark brownish complexion that clearly indicated mixture.

This stocky built valorous man regulated the boys 'home in a manner that all soldiers could respect. If he had drama or misunderstandings with wards, or his staff, he would personally take them to the backyard shed and physically handles his business. He expected the wards to do the same amongst each other. There we had summer jobs earning $130 every two weeks for doing chores around the houses. To compare these two adjoining houses, to the average house in Watts would have you believing they were mansions. They were two stories tall with each one of them holding five bedrooms.

There was another counselor who I remember vividly because he was a malfeasant individual. He sold weed to the wards when we got paid from our summer jobs. The first time I bought a $10 sack of weed from him he said, "I'm selling it to you today, and I'm busting you tomorrow." I thought to myself, "Damn, that's hypocritical." I assumed that that was his way of saying don't take him for granted or front him off.

One day this little fat ass Crip named Mitchell and I were arguing in the house. We were both fourteen years old. Mr. Woods heard us and said, "Come with me." He escorted us to the backyard shed and said, "Go ahead and fight." Fat-ass and I put up our fists, in a fighting stance, and were waiting for each other to throw the first punch. Finally, I hit him in his fat cheekbone. He stood there looking stupid. I noticed he was afraid and I took advantage of it and I popped him two more times in his jaw. He started crying. Mr. Woods then escorted us back to the house as he taunted fat-boy and told him that he didn't want to hear his mouth anymore. After that I kind of sensed Mr. Woods had respect for my young courage of being a Blood and out-numbered by the Crips, though he never said anything about it to me. But the ironic thing about Mitchell—he still talked shit to me as though he had won the fight, or at least he fought me back. A week later I had another fight with a young Crip named Kenney-T.

His brother was also in the home. I also found it very ironic that he wanted to fight me as well. Word amongst the wards was he got caught performing perverted favors on another young Crip ward. And now he wanted to fight me like he was a gangbanger who was conducting himself in a formal manner. We stepped to the backyard, which was a hard dirt surface. No counselors were present on this evening.

The fight began and we both started hitting each other in our facial area. He was doing pretty good despite the stigma. The fight turned into a wrestling match. I was on top of him. There were all the Crips and Jasper's scary ass watching the fight. I don't know where Larry was hiding. While I was on top of him, the Crips ran over and started hitting me on my head.

I felt knuckles coming from everywhere, but I somehow made it back to my feet and ran to the bus stop. I waited for the bus to come and pick me up. I was tired of those dudes jumping on folks. My mind was made up. I was going back to my neighborhood to get a gun and come back and shoot-up that whole boys' home. As I waited I looked around and here comes a Crip named John Berry a.k.a. Bull—and was built like one too. He had taken a liking towards me. His intentions were to persuade me into going back to the home with him. he assured me that he would give me support. I told Bull, "I will fight any Crip in the home as long as it's one-on-one." Bull was from Harlem 30's.

West Marlin Boys' Home decided to send me to another boys' home for no reason other than being a suspect of breaking into a local liquor store.

In December 1974, I was placed in the Ferguson's Boys' Home. That home was much more peaceful than the other two. The Crips there weren't too much into the gangbanging lifestyle. I only stayed there for nine days. The counselor would let us go home to visit with our families for a three day Christmas visit.

The Ferguson home fed us out of the same plates they fed the dogs. I didn't like it one bit while I was there, but I couldn't do anything about it. So I took advantage of what I thought could be a morbid situation. I told my probation officer I wasn't going back to the home because we were being fed from the same dishes as the dogs. I stood firm on my belief that this was a health risk. Surprisingly, my probation officer allowed me to stay home, without serious concerns that I was trying to manipulate myself out of not completing the few months that I had left to serve. I was grateful, but again I continued my blight of destruction.

A few months later my criminal behavior landed me in juvenile hall again for burglary. Shortly thereafter, I was found guilty and convicted to serve the expected six-month-term in county camp. On April 25, 1975, I was placed in Camp Kilpatrick. I served beyond the six months due to bad conduct and was forced to remain there for eleven months. Camp Kilpatrick was dubbed the rowdiest of all camps. Failing to meet their expectations would require Youth Authority Placement (YAP).

They had a point based system program which each staff who worked the dormitory scored the wards daily behavior from zero to five. The following day the point's sheet would be placed on the recreation room wall, so that all the wards could see their scores from yesterday's deeds. This point system would determine when a ward goes home. It may be an early, expected, or a later release date. I participated in a couple of fights, and then I decided I wanted to do the necessary things to go home. I was determined to earn the highest points. One morning I went to look at the scores, and became so enraged that I couldn't keep my actions in check. I grabbed a metal trash can and threw it at Counselor Takens as he stood in the center of the podium, in the dormitory, for giving me a two-point score when I believe to have earned a five, considering all of the extra deeds I had done that day.

In retrospect what I hadn't realized was that I allowed one minute of anger to scourge me to stay in camp for extra months, when my goal was to get out in a suitable time. Fortunately, for Counselor Takens, he'd knocked it down in mid air before it hit him. I was punished to remain in the hole (confinement) for a month.

I couldn't imagine the stress that I had put my mother through. I prayed to God that he would bless me with an opportunity to make a positive change, and meaningful achievements in my life.

My juvenile criminal history consisted of merely fifty arrests. The local police-department constantly raided my mother's home. It became so bad that I had established such an infamous reputation with the Firestone police-department. When a crime was committed, I was the police's prime suspect. Even when I had no involvement, my mother's home would still be intruded.

Eventually, I completed the Camp Kilpatrick program and was released to my mother. Deep inside of my young heart, I wanted to do right, but it seemed as though I just couldn't stay out of people houses. This was the only way we could get guns. I often went into houses while the residents slept. I had even been in someone's home and saw them come in and walked through the front door while I was in their bedroom. It scared the shit out of me, but it didn't deter me. I was aware of the fact that burglars had been killed while in other people's homes.

After being released from Camp Kilpatrick for about six months, I was arrested again and had to go through the juvenile hall process. The results put me in the Camp Gonzales county program for another burglary offense. There I was in Los Padrino (LP) Juvenile Hall reception center.

This juvenile facility was cell-designed, though there were some small dormitories in certain units. I was placed in unit C-D, which were cells as small as seven by ten feet, with no sink or toilet, just a small stool and desk mounted to the wall, and a metal spring bunk at the rear of the cell. These were some depressing living conditions, you had to pound on the cell door to get the counselor's attention, so that you could come out to use the bathroom.

During the evening dayroom period while we were waiting for chow, we had to align ourselves in two lines (side-by-side) to walk to the mess-hall.

I was observing the wards in the dayroom and two guys stood out as the most dominant of all the wards. They both appeared to be very closely acquainted to each other. Both of their names were Wolf, as Mexicans from Pico Viejo and a Crip from the east coast who was black. He would later be dubbed Ronnie-Bam, one of Raymond's first five Crips and founder of east coast Crips. These two wards were the biggest in the dayroom, each holding seventeen inch arms.

They horse-played with each other in a rowdy, but friendly manner that no other wards dared to feel the privilege to participate in their playful activities. I didn't' know neither of them, but I was fascinated by their robust and courageous personas.

So, my endeavor was to be-friend them, I made playful gestures towards them and the both of them looked at me as though I was some kind of groupie or something. I clearly sensed the negative vibe that my friend was unwanted. A couple of hours later we formed lines, and walked to the mess-hall.

Mexican Wolf was walking on the side of me in the opposite line. I made another friendly comment, I guess by now I had become annoying. He blurted, "Shut the fuck up!" So I did. But I've always been an obstinate lad. As we entered the mess-hall and prepared to sit down, waiting for the counselor's command to sit at the tables, I said to Wolf in a jovial tone, "What's up, S.A.?"

Wolf became irate and spluttered something in discontent as he set in motion to swing at me. Before he could bring his fists up in full swinging position, I hit him so fast and hard with about seven consecutive blows of lefts and rights within perhaps two seconds, literally. All Wolf could do was say "Ay, yi yi!" (A Spanish expression of damn) as he dropped his head in shock. The counselors took us to the hole for seventy-two hours. Wolf threatened me over the tier through the cell doors that he was going to kick my ass when we got out of the hole. I laughed, and replied, "I'ma beat your ass again!"

What Wolf failed to recognize was that I wasn't trying to be friend them out of cowardice. I respected their rowdiness, because I was rowdy, and wanted to associate myself with strength.

Upon completing our seventy-two hours confinement, the counselor called Wolf and me to his office separately to speak with us before letting us back to the unit. We both gave him our word that there would be no future problems between the two of us. And we held on to our words. I gave Wolf a nasty black eye that covered his entire eye down to the bottom of his nose. It was black and bloodshot red. I noticed that both of the Wolf's recognized my Ridahism, though we remained aloof.

Three months later, Mexican Wolf and I, would be together again in Camp Gonzalez. On this occasion we became friends. I saw him fight twice there, with a Crip and a Mexican gang member who was an enemy of his gang.

Both of Wolf's fights were hard-blow-throwing toe-to-toe. Judging by Wolf's performance on both of his fights, he we went toe-to-toe he had the potentials to whip me, or at the least make a good fight.

I have heard from one of Wolf's homeboys from his set that he was killed many years ago by a rival gang member.

I would also encounter Wolf-Ronnie-Bam again many years later, on a San Quentin prison yard amongst many other Crips. he has been in prison for just as long as I have been, but my prison activities far exceed his. Though according to my knowledge, his name remains unimpaired amongst 33 the gang society. Had it not, I'm confident that I would have heard something, being that most of these dudes in prison are very loquacious. The gossip more than Barbara Walters, and "The View."

On November 30, 1976, I was sentenced to serve a six-month term at Camp Gonzalez. Having been through all of the boys' homes and camps, I had learned to do the necessary things to complete the programs. However, I got into a couple of fights, but this time I completed the program in nine months. Two months earlier than I completed Camp Kilpatrick program.

One fight I remember was with this tall light-skinned Crip. I didn't know his name, but I knew his accomplice very well. He was Motor-Mouse from Rollin' Sixties Crips. the other guy and I decided we would play tunk (cards) for cosmetics. Motor-Mouse was sitting next to me like he wasn't involved and playing the neutral role. He would ask to see my hand on every play. I couldn't understand why the dude I gambled with would fall and consecutively win, as though he could see through my cards. He had nearly won everything in my locker. Briefly I had looked down towards the floor and surprisingly saw Motor-Mouse's foot, touching and hitting the gambler's foot, giving him a signal to fall.

I quickly jumped to my feet and said, "Nigga, you ain't getting anything from me!" He jumped up, and we start fighting. We threw a few punches and the counselor came and broke it up.

A few months after that incident, I was released again to my mother. I unfortunately continued my criminal path of conduct. In 1977, I was committed to the California's Youth Authority (CYA) for another burglary. I was sentenced to serve ten months in custody. First, I went to the Norwalk CYA reception center, enroute to be placed at a more settled institution. Norwalk officials decided that they'd send me to CYA Paso Robles to serve my time, after examining me and my case for a few months.

During my first week at Paso, I engaged in an unforgettable fight with a white kid. I was sixteen years old. And I'm sure he was around this same age, being that these institutions are established based upon age. This white guy was kind of buff. His arms were about fifteen-inches wide. During this era in CYA that was a size to be reckoned with. I held my average thirteen-inch arms. The dormitory that we were in held thirty wards. Fifteen bunks lined up on both sides of the walls, with a walkway between the bunks. My bunk was next to this buff guy.

I basically provoked this white guy into damn near knocking me out. For no reason whatsoever,

I wanted to fight him. We were sitting on our bunks facing each other. I was persistent in trying to get him to go into a room to fight me. He obviously didn't want any problems with me. I assumed he thought I was an enigmatic person.

Because I gave him no alternative but to fight. For a brief second, I put my head down, and he hit me so hard. I saw so many starts it was incredible that this white boy had the audacity to hit me! He was so afraid or angry that it gave him an edge. He hit me with about six more consecutive blows.

All I could do was grab him before he knocked me out. I regained my senses and started hitting him back. By this time, the counselors ran over to stop it. And Larry, who was at the West Marlin's Boys' Home with me, grabbed me and said, "Be cool, before you catch more time!" but I continued to break away from his grasp as well as the counselors. I never made contact with the guy due to the continuous grabbing that later subdued me. I was sent to the hole for refusing to stop fighting, when it should have been over. Paso Robles had a confinement program that consisted of levels of completions to graduate. The program required a three-month period of no misconduct reports. Upon completion of the first level, one would receive a red stamp.

The second month, a person would receive a blue stamp. The third month offered a green stamp.

In return, the ward would be released from confinement.

If a person received any misconduct reports, he was obligated to start all over again. I had a very difficult time trying to complete this program.

I can vividly recall the sincerity of a Mexican counselor named Mr. Roberson waiting to help me complete a "stamp" level. He would bring me a cake of my choice after having his wife bake it. His concern and offer prompted me to make an effort to complete the program. When I got close to completion, I would have a fight.

All of my life I've had the spirit of a rebel. In confinement we lived in one man cells. When we went to the showers, we would shower on the same side that our cell was on.

There were ten cells on both sides of the corridor facing each other. Where you could look out of your door window and see the ward in his cell across from you through the windows. Across from me was a Crip kid named Blue, and his neighbor was Tiaras who said he was an ex-Blood. To consider one an ex-gang member at that young age is considered a cowardly act. But Tiaras appeared to have been solid. During a shower period I noticed Blue had a birth mark on the side of his buttock. I started teasing him, and dubbed him "Cherry Thang." Tiaras and I used to team up on Blue something fierce. Tiaras even made a blues song called "Cherry Thang."

Blue got tired of us teasing him, and finally challenged me to a fight. We fought in the recreation room, blow-for-blow. And by the look of him, I underestimated his ability. Our bout was perhaps a draw. But the fight didn't deter me from teasing him. tiaras and I continued teasing him. This was the best pastime in those cells for kids.

Jebb was the only white kid in the hole at this time. A couple of white counselors loved Jebb. He was a courageous kid, who looked like a young hillbilly. One day, Jebb and I had a very minute disagreement that wasn't worth thinking about in fighting terms. When our doors were unlocked to come out of our cells, we had to stand in front of our cell doors, until the counselor instructed us to form a line.

Then we would be escorted to our intended schedules as the evening showers were being conducted.

I was casually walking in back of Jebb, and as soon as we made our way inside the shower room he turned around and socked me directly in the mouth, busting my lip. Before I could react, the counselors were right there to stop it as I struggled to fight back.

Jebb and I went to the hole, which was a hole within the hole for those of us who were under this confinement program. Jeb stayed for twenty-four hours and seventy-two hours had passed before I was freed. The same day I got out of the hole we attended school.

Our doors were opened, and we begin to line up in front of our cells. Before we could form a line, I took off after Jebb like a madman! We started socking each other in the face. The counselors quickly broke it up, but I was the one who was being restrained, which allowed Jebb to get in a couple of good blows. When they brought the fight under control, I noticed Jebb's lip was bleeding. I was content. After eleven months, the Paso Robles officials decided they'd place me in a higher custody of the CYA. So, they transferred me to Youth Training School (YTS). The architectural design was that of cells. There were many units and being two stories, but totally different modules. Each unit was named alphabetically.

My unit was W&X. this particular building was considered the most active for gangbangers. I noticed that the Bloods there were more courageous than those in the boys' homes, camps, or youth authority I had been in. I've always possessed a keen awareness of my environment and could determine the character and abilities of other wards. Often, I am correct.

There was a Blood named Ness from VNG (Van Ness Gangsta). He appeared to have a big mouth, but not in a disrespectful manner but an exuberant one. He stood out amongst all of the wards in the recreation room. I had just turned seventeen, and Ness was twenty-one years old. I figured he wasn't genuinely valorous.

One afternoon while in the recreation room, Ness and the biggest Blood I had ever seen, in any juvenile placement, engaged in an argument. The blood's name was Larry Beam. He was from Lueders Park Piru (LPP).

Beam was about 6'3" and 230 pounds. He held twenty-inch arms and a solid physique. Ness was around 5'8", and 180 pounds, without a muscular physique.

They were both in each other's face, engaging in a heated verbal confrontation. Beam walked away suddenly to go use the bathroom. As he exited the dayroom (recreation room), Ness angrily blurted to a group of wards at the table, "If he gets in my face again, I'ma fire on his ass!"

Beam came back and went directly to Ness to resume their argument. Ness reached up to the towering Beam's face and punched him in his jaw. Beam then started throwing Ness all around the dayroom, as if he were a rag-doll. The counselors came running into the dayroom and pulled Beam off of Ness. It was then when I realized that Ness's heart was equal to his character.

I noticed another Blood named Peabody who was very popular. He went home after my first week there. But in that brief period, he appeared to be kissing the Crips' asses and going out of his way to please then. Some Bloods were angry that he gave his TV and radio to a lil' Crip named Pinky, from Rollin' Sixties, when he went home. I heard that the lil' brother, Pinky, was gunned down and killed shortly after he was released from YTS. He was a young trooper. May his soul rest in peace.

I participated in a few fights. The one I recall most was with a Crip named Red. One afternoon in the dayroom while playing cards at the table with a group of wards, Red and I started arguing over a play I made. At this point, I wasn't familiar with the ward's code.

Red said to me, "We can go into the laundry room and fight." The laundry room was an isolated area where wards could fight without the counselor's knowledge.

When he challenged me, I couldn't display any signs of cowardice. Though I was nervous because e was much bigger than me, I said, "All right." He left the dayroom and walked towards the laundry room.

I followed him, nervous but willing. When we reached the laundry room, the door was locked. I turned around and walked away. I was relieved, but Red asked, "Where are you going? I'm going to go through the bathroom window and open the door for you!" he said. So I stayed near, waiting to fight him. the bathroom and laundry room were adjoined. He went in the bathroom, jumped through the window, and opened the door for me. I went inside. The fool was determined to get me inside the laundry room. I should have known he had skills.

He threw the first blows, hitting me in my face several times before I could react. I started fighting back, but it was no avail. It was like that big ass Lennox Lewis on Tyson. This fool was hitting me so hard that I started to swing with my head down, to avoid some of them blows. I grabbed him, during the wrestling and punched him upside his head as hard as I could. Red had stop struggling at the point, so he said, "Oh, you wanna keep going huh?" I didn't answer, but my pantomime clearly stated, "Hell naw!" So the fight ended with that punch.

Then we left the laundry room. The next day I went to the infirmary to get treatment for my battle wounds. They put a cast on my right-hand. I had broken it on the last blow. I had a knot in the middle of my forehead, swelling on both sides of my nose, and two black eyes.

I was in a mess and was more embarrassed than I was in actual pain. But what really aggravated me the most was the dude clearly whipped me, yet lied and told all the other wards I broke my hand hitting the shelf. I thought to myself, "This bitch nigga can't keep it authentic!" My Crip partner named Pete from Compton let me wear his murder-ones (sunglasses) to conceal my bruised eyes, but the staff knew I had been in a physical altercation. One of them made a sarcastic remark about my face. I took offense to it and spit in his face. They sent me to confinement which was C&D unit. After that brutal incident, one thing I learned for certain was that no matter how hard a mutha fucker is hitting, I had to keep my head up.

Knuckles are going to hurt no matter if a person's head is up or down. It is to my advantage to have my head up, looking at what's going on. And perhaps I could have avoided some of those blows. I learned from that experience. To this very day, currently at forty-eight years old. I've never fought in that manner.

Approximately seven months were left before I was to be released. I kind of put my heart in check and accepted small insults that I wouldn't ordinarily accept. My primary goal was to get out of YTS.

I had every intention of doing the right thing, once I was released. I made it home. I did two years instead of the ten-months I was sentenced to. For a month or so I avoided going in the neighborhood areas where I knew the only goals in my life would be to hang out or do negative things.

So I basically stayed home, other than going to the store and back. I even cut grass for one of my mother's friends who lived across the tracks in a Crip neighborhood. She was my mother's elderly church member.

Before this I had never done legal work other than painting houses and being a paper-boy very briefly with my elder brother, Earl.

I went to cut her grass at 8 A.M. and finished at about 8 P.M. I mean it was literally hard labor, because the old lady was very meticulous. She had me doing all kind of things, that weren't necessary. If she noticed one piece of grass out of place she would have me pick it out.

I stayed much longer than I expected. When she finally allowed me to leave, she gave me thirty-five cents. I thought, "Damn! I was at least expecting ten dollars. I could have just done this work as a good deed and it would have felt better than receiving thirty-five cents."

Shortly after this discouraging experience of trying to do the right thing and working, my cousin came over to my house one night. This nut had the audacity to ask me if I wanted to do a neighborhood burglary with him.

And I call him "Nut" because every time I went to jail, I would be oblivious to him in all ways you can imagine. Then, when I got out of jail, he would be the first person to put weed or sherm (PCP) in my mouth. He would urge me to violate the law in some way or the other. I agreed to commit the burglary with him, and we were on our way. Half way down the block my conscience and recidivistic behavior was battling. I said to him, "No, I ain't going." And I turned around and went back home. My cousin had carried out the burglary. Perhaps five hours later a police car drove up to my mother's house.

My mother let the policeman In the house and he said I was under arrest for burglary. He handcuffed me and escorted me to the police car. I had just turned eighteen years old. I was headed to the Los Angeles County Jail, for the first time.

After serving many months and years as a juvenile delinquent, I accepted responsibility for my own actions. I didn't cry about whatever penalty that I was scourge to endure, but being charged for something that I whole-heartedly avoided made my hateful attitude towards the police increase.

I was booked in the LA County Jail, and remained there for seven days. On the seventh day I was unexpectedly released without notification of a court hearing, or otherwise. I never understood or knew why the charges were dropped, but I was elated to be back out, especially because I didn't commit the offense. Shortly after I got out of the county jail, I started mingling with the ominous in-crowd in my 'hood. And the contrary thing was, I was trying to avoid a neighborhood that I was the bad influence on.

In most cases, I was the regulator who inspired those who I hung with to err. I knew if I went back to the neighborhood, my future wouldn't be so pleasant. Nevertheless, all of my homeboys embraced me.

I noticed there was a new face in the 'hood and, I was concerned about the manner in which he blended in with my homies since I had never seen him before. I assumed he was a Bishop, but one of my homies informed me that dude was a Crip.

With me being involved in so much gang activity in boys' homes, county camps, and CYAs, I couldn't understand how these Bloods just let a Crip exist in the neighborhood. His name was Mike. He was the boyfriend of one of my reputable big homie's sister. That was the only reason he was allowed to come and hang out in our neighborhood as he pleased. I observed this dude for about a week, and he was a jacker (robber). We started hanging out with one another. Therefore, my burglaries would become obsolete. One day Mike and I went to Mike's sister's house. She lived with about four other homegirls from the 'hood. The three of us went to a hamburger stand to get a bite to eat. That same night Mike's sister, Sheryl became my girlfriend.

Sheryl was the second and last girlfriend I ever had. I got the coochie that same night. Mike, Sheryl, and I slept in my bedroom. Sheryl had the bed, while Mike and I slept on the floor. At around 12 P.M. I noticed Mike was asleep, and then I made my move on Sheryl, and started fondling and caressing her. Suddenly, she awakened and offered me to come and lay in her bed with her. I was eighteen and she was twenty-two. She had much more experience than I had.

I recall once driving my cousin Verna to the Martin Luther King Hospital for medical complications with her two-years-old son, O.J. I vividly remember Diana Ross' hit record "My House" coming on the radio. Verna immediately directed me to a record store so that she could purchase that album. As I drove, Sheryl looked at me in a discontented manner and said, "I'm going to buy you some gin." I had no idea what she was insinuating, because I wasn't a drinker. Many years later in prison I had learned what she was trying to point out to me. One day while having a conversation with some homies on the yard, I enlightened them to what she had said to me. They laughed, and the homie, Ruboi from Skyline Piru, said, "You didn't have enough stamina for her. Gin gives you lasting ability and an erection."

I really liked Sheryl, but never displayed any real affection toward her. Our relationship strengthened the bond between Mike and me. The girl was charming. In a short time she won over my mom and family and basically moved into our home until she allegedly cheated on me with my cousin, Edward. To this very day I'm not sure if it really happened or not, but the circumstances were this, I had been smoking sherm (PCP) that night and was feeling terribly bad, and having severe headaches and confusion of thoughts.

My sisters, Patricia, and Elizabeth, and my cousins, Verna, Edward, and my girlfriend Sheryl were at my house planning to go to the Sunday night club in the neighborhood. They asked me if I wanted to go along with them. But I declined due to my drugged-out condition. Sheryl was animated about staying home with me, but I insisted that she go with them to have an innocent, but good time. I didn't see any detrimental reason why she couldn't go and party with my family. So they went about their way. And I immediately fell into a deep sleep. The following morning I woke up and felt refreshed.

Therefore, I implemented my morning rituals, and drove over to Verna's house, who lived around the corner. I arrived around 10 or 11 A.M. that Monday morning, and she was the only person home.

Verna enlightened me on some disturbing news she had, and then informed me that she had seen Edward and Sheryl together that morning were walking down the street of Firestone Boulevard.

As though they were coming from a motel. Sheryl came over to Verna's house later that day. I confronted her with the information I'd heard, and my suspicions of her and Edward's affair.

She strongly denied it and started crying vehemently, and begging me not to break-up with her, while on her knees. Verna provided me with the information, but then began showing sympathy for the weeping Sheryl. She even asked me to give Sheryl a second chance and said that perhaps she could have made a misjudgment. Even though Verna had always been the big sister figure to us all, I was stern with my decision on leaving Sheryl. At that period of my eighteen years of life, I couldn't even spell the word fidelity, but the intuition that dwelled within me had always been faithful to whatever I devoted myself to.

As I narrate my experiences and trials-and-tribulations I do not promote the usage of any form of illegal drugs. In fact, I am anti-drugs. It has to some degree or another destroyed many of our lives.

Rather it is the retardation of the mental capacity, or physical impairment. In many instances when we act under the influence of drugs, it is an artificial mindset.

And once we, who are fortunate enough to talk about it, or regain our normal thinking pattern, then we are left with serious regrets or problems. As I have been suffering from, for over three decades (30 years) and still counting.

During that time, I continued to be a menace to society. However, my final act of disruption in society happened when Mike and I decided to plan a robbery. We were at the neighborhood's liquor store and unexpectedly saw an old friend of mine. His name was Clyde.

I had known him for quite awhile and somewhat admired his reputation as a Blood. When I was eleven 43 years old he pulled a gun out on me in a manner gesturing that he would shoot me. He was an original Bounty Hunter, but later turned Alley Bishop. The three of us started conversing about the robbery and Clyde decided he would join us in this plot. We headed to the local neighborhood drug-dealer to buy a twenty dollar stick of sherm (PCP).

We smoked the stick and were high as hell. I felt that we could conquer anything. We spotted two Cubans who were intoxicated, and coming out of a bar.

Anyone who we believed had money could have been our victims. We stalked them to their house. As we entered the backyard, I pulled out my .22 caliber long barrel western movie looking handgun. One of the victims was so nervous he attempted to knock the weapon from my hand. But the gun went off and hit him in the chest. I then saw them flee towards their house. We never thought that a robbery would turn lethal. After the resonating sounds from the boisterous gun firing, we ran away. The three of us disbursed into separate directions. About a month after the shooting, I was once again at the local liquor store. This time I was accompanied by my pimp demeanor type of homeboy, Martin Jr.

I observed two police cars driving slowly down the busy street of Firestone Boulevard.

The police cars turned down the street that I resided on. I nervously said to Martin, "I bet they are going to my house!" I ran down the street they had turned on. Indeed, my predication was correct. I ran back to Martin and told him I was right. I went in the liquor store's phone booth and I called my mother. The police officer answered the phone. I told him who I was. He said he would like to talk to me about a murder, and I should come home and talk to him. I thought to myself, "You're crazy than a mutha fucker." But I told him I would be right there in a few minutes.

"Don't go anywhere," I said.

Martin and I quickly left the neighborhood and we went to his sister, Clarisse's house. She lived across the tracks in the Crip's neighborhood. It was about 10 or 11 P.M.

I knew Martin's sister. She was pretty. I wanted to get in her panties while I was in the sixth grade. She welcomed us into her home. She lived with her boyfriend, John, who was my homeboy from my gang. He was on his way to work as we walked in. We chatted briefly, and then he left. Martin said he was going to go back to our 'hood to see what the police were doing at my house. I

35

attempted to go with him, but he said he felt it would be best that I stay put. But I insisted that I go. Clarisse said, "You can stay here with me, I ain't gonna bite you!"

So I went back to my seat. Martin left, leaving me and the lady to ourselves. She wasn't the little exquisite girl I once desired. Now she's 5'7" in height and perhaps 230 pounds, but still she possessed her pretty face. Imagine the face of singer T-Boz (TLC) on a fat-Star-Jones's body. I was sitting in a kitchen chair. The kitchen and living room were adjoined with a clear open view.

I sat there for about thirty minutes. It appeared that she was waiting for me to make a move on her. But I was afraid. I thought to myself, "Shit, the police is looking for me, on murder charges. I'm subject to be in jail any day. I better get this coochie." By this time, she had drifted off into a light sleep.

Finally, I mustered enough courage to walk over to the couch where she laid. I gently reached down and started pulling down her big, tight ass panties.

She suddenly awoke as though she were astounded. Clarisse grabbed me by the head, and pulled me closed to her. Then started kissing me while pulling down her panties simultaneously.

As we begin to get it on, she kept reiterating, "Faster-faster-faster!" in her rapid feminine tone.

She said it throughout our—perhaps five or ten minute session.

When I was done, I quickly went into the bathroom to wash myself. I remained for maybe five minutes. When I returned, John was in the living room. I wondered had he been spying on us by looking through the living room window. He never questioned me about the event, but I'm sure he wouldn't because he was meddling around with some of the other lil' homegirls in the 'hood. And she knew about his infidelity.

That night I slept on the couch. The next day I went back to my neighborhood with Martin. I felt confused and didn't know what I should do. One thing I knew for certain was that it wasn't safe to remain in my 'hood. I mustered up $200. That night I got on a plane and flew back to Louisiana.

Chapter 2

A One Way Ticket to Captivity

When I arrived in Louisiana, my first cousin, Linda was at the airport waiting for me. Everything felt so foreign. I had never traveled no farther than California. She took me to her home. She lived in a large trailer-home with her husband and two young boys. She lived in Bossier City, the rural area. I felt uncomfortable for a few days.

Gradually, I blended in with the family. I didn't feel like a total stranger because I knew her as my biological relative. I knew that my blood was going to love me no matter what, in most cases. At least that's what my young mind believed. During the entire three months I spent with my cousin and father, I never felt completely at ease.

While in Louisiana, I met the lady who took care of the family before I was born. She and her late husband, Butter-Ball who I've heard so much about from my mother, were the closest relatives that I have known to being a grandmother and grandfather. Butter-Ball had died many years ago. I would have been very pleased to have met him. I was told I was his favorite kid. And he wanted to keep me in Louisiana with him when my mother left for California. But she didn't allow me to stay. The next day Linda called my father to let him know that I was in town. He lived in the city district. He told Linda that he would be over to pick me up the following day. However, he didn't show up. The first thought that came to my mind was, "The fool ain't claiming me, like so many black men in the depressed ass country for a black man." I was surprised when he showed up the next day after he was supposed to have come.

At age 18, I saw my biological father for the first time. When I saw him, I immediately noticed the resemblance. I knew where I got my hazel-eyes from. He took me to his house to meet his wife and my two older brothers and sister.

It surprised me to know my father had the demeanor similar to that of a player. He had three girlfriends. All of them lived in this home-town. And one of them even lived about five houses down from him. on the same side of the street. Nevertheless, he was married. And he felt guilt in his actions.

He once told me, "I love my wife, she is good to me and puts up with the mess I do." My father and I went to the neighborhood's liquor store. As we got out the car there were about four guys standing in front of the store. One of them yelled over to us, "Hey, Red-Shirt, that's your son?"

My father replied, "Yeah." Obviously the guy saw the strikingly resemblance. He took me over to all of his girlfriends' houses. They all had daughters in my age group. Some of them were fine as hell.

I sensed that some liked me, but I lacked the courage of being aggressive in going after females. In retrospect, my shyness and lack of aggression towards females caused me to miss out on a lot of coochie.

Shit, maybe that's a good thing.

Especially in these days, there are too many diseases and epidemics in our communities. I never experienced a sexual disease of any kind whatsoever. So to say that, some good came out of my nearly absent sexual affairs. But during my youth, I resented that aspect of my characteristics. I vividly recall a time when my father took me to work with him. After work, we went to pick up one of his girlfriends from her job.

We drove around certain parts of the city. My father said to his girlfriend that he was going to take me home. She said in a sincere voice, "Let him stay with us." They briefly conversed about it and he prevailed. He took her home first to prevent his wife or neighbors from seeing her when he dropped me off.

While taking me home, he said in his rapidly speaking voice, "I don't know what she's talking about. I'm taking you home, so I can go back and get me some pussy." I found that to be shocking and boisterously funny.

Old pop's was dead serious about going back and getting that coochie. He was nowhere near being shy when it was concerning women. I went to a few clubs with my brothers. They were both cool in their own ways. The oldest was Poochie. He was 29. Johnny Ray was 23.

All three of us had different mothers. Poochie's biological mother was married to my father, up until he passed away in 1995. Poochie was basically an alcoholic. He just lived from day-to-day just to get his drink on. Johnny Ray had a player type of demeanor.

When we went clubbing he would get on the dance floor and his pantomime were as though he's clearly indicating to the female that he's finer and sexier than she was. One night we went to a club and we were all drinking and having fun.

When we made it home around midnight, as we got out of the car, for no apparent reason, Johnny Ray grabbed Poochie by his shirt collar and started manhandling him.

Poochie was far more befuddled than we were. We went into the house. Johnny Ray sat down on the living room sofa. Poochie went into the kitchen. Something within told me to go see if he all right.

I walked into the kitchen and there was Poochie holding a long ass butcher knife in his hand. I asked him, "What are you going to do with that?" "Get him," he said in his drunken demeanor.

I said, "That's your brother."

And I took the knife away from him. We walked into the living room. Poochie walked casually over to Johnny Ray as though his purpose was just to pass by him to go up-stairs.

Johnny Ray was still sitting on the sofa. Poochie stopped in front of Johnny Ray and socked him in his face extremely hard. And he immediately started to run up-stairs. Johnny Ray grabbed one of his legs, but Poochie somehow struggled himself free and fled up-stairs. The loud commotion woke everyone in the house. Everyone came running into the living room. Johnny Ray started crying as he wasn't anticipating this result. My stepsister, Caroline was very angry at Johnny Ray. She blurted, "He's supposed to be my brother and he tried to fuck me!"

My father made the notion that he wasn't surprised or it wasn't a sin, being that there was no blood relation. I don't blame him either. She was a smooth chocolate complexion. Fine features, and a nice curvy physique.

I once came in one late night, and she was sleeping on the couch. She had on a see through negligee displaying her red panties. I too had some ogling eyes, but I kept my behavior in check.

Everything simmered down, and Johnny Ray went home. He lived around the corner with his aunt. The next morning, Poochie told me Johnny Ray had never done anything like that to him until I came around.

A couple of weeks later, while I was in Bossier City, my father were informed that the police had been there to his house looking for me. He took me back to Linda's house in the country. When we arrived, Linda and other family and friends were standing out front of the trailer home, they appeared to be in dismay.

Linda said the police had just left from there, too. She encouraged me to turn myself over to the authority so that they may be lenient with me. Not knowing that this would be a "one-way ticket to captivity," for me. I agreed. I never revealed to Linda or my father that I was a fugitive.

She called the police. About thirty minutes later they came back to apprehend me. They took me to the Bossier City County Jail. After about five minutes of standing at the counter being booked, I asked a black police officer if I could smoke a cigarette. He said, "Yeah," so I fired up a Kool. As I stood smoking my cigarette some funny looking white police officer emerged from an office.

This guy looked like the dude, Michael, from the popular sitcom "All in the Family." He told me to put the cigarette out before he smashed it out on my ass. I remembered as a kid learning about how racist white people were in Louisiana. So, I thought he was one of those deep-down-south rednecks.

They put me in a caged that consisted of four cells, with six-men per cell. It appeared that whites and blacks functioned as one in this jail, prisoners against the guards. The same deputy who displayed a hardcore attitude towards me, the prisoners were talking to him like we was some kind of dweeb. I thought to myself, "This fool was perpetrating—coward ass mutha fucka!"

Within a few days of being in Bossier County Jail, the Los Angeles detective arrived to question me on the murder charges. He asked me, what I knew about a murder and robbery that took place on Lou Dillion Street? Told him, "I don't know anything about it." I was confident that when all was done, I would be vindicated. The detective saw that he couldn't get any information from me. So, he said, "Hayes and Simmons said you were the triggerman." I laughed at him in contempt. I knew the manipulating games policemen played to obtain information that they needed.

He said, "Okay, then listen." He played their confession on his cassette player. Those bastards had ratted on me like they were Sammy The Bull, the infamous mafia underboss who turned informant on the late mafia family boss, John Gotti.

My heart subsided so deep into depression, I knew I was doomed, but I stuck to my plea. I didn't want to stay in Louisiana's County Jail.

On December 7, 1979, I was extradited from the Bossier City County Jail to the Los Angeles County Jail. Two undercover-detectives escorted me to the airport, by way of; I believe a rental-car.

Because the car was left at the airport. They handcuffed me in a covert manner. Only one hand was cuffed as I walked in the middle of them. To where they had my hand in some kind of slipknot that could quickly unleash me and put them back on. Every time the stewardess observed the handcuffs, the officers would quickly let loose my hand. Because of this, I assumed it was illegal for law-enforcement agencies to transport an arrested felon on public airplanes.

I didn't know. It was just an assumption I had, due to their deceitful conduct aboard the plane.

The next day the detectives and I arrived back in California. I first went to some substation in Los Angeles County Jail where I was booked on a murder charge. I lay back quietly and contemplated on my situation for about a week or so. Shortly thereafter, I was called for a court appearance. My state-appointed lawyer said this was just a procedure intended to weigh the evidence to see if the case was strong enough to be bound over to superior court. My preliminary hearing was set to begin in a month. I went back in that month and was quickly bound over to stand trial for murder and robbery.

A trial date was scheduled. I remained in LA County Jail for eleven months. I was fighting a murder charge with a public defender who wasn't putting up much of a fight for me. A few months went by, and I started to realize that this prison shit may be my life. I eventually started to engage in the same type of behavior I had participated in all of my life. The officials moved me to a permanent module. The unit was 22-24 hundred.

Everyone was programming in the dayroom when I arrived. The police instructed me to put my linen in my assigned cell and take it to the dayroom with the other blues. That was a term they called prisoners.

When I entered the dayroom I \observed Mexicans, Whites, and Blacks in there. Five blacks were sitting and conversing with one another. I quizzed them all.

I went down the line, "Where you from?" the first one said, "Rollin' Sixty Crip." The next guy was a "Harlem Crip, another was a "Hoover Crip," and one was a "Compton Crip." So I assumed the last one was a Crip, too.

"So you're a Crip, too, huh?" I asked.

He said in a hesitant manner, "No, I'm a Denver Lane."

I eagerly stated, "I ma Blood too, man! I just moved in cell-13!"

He said that he was in the same cell. I knew the Crips didn't like my bold approach the way I came into that dayroom quizzing folks, but I didn't give a damn. I have never been a scary dude.

The deputies conducted dayroom recall. All the prisoners went back to their cells. I walk into my new cell, and there were two other blacks assigned to the cell, one Mexican-looking Cuban, two Mexicans, and me. We all shared this six-man cell. The brothers introduced themselves to me. The one who was in the dayroom when I arrived said his name was Peabody from Denver Lane. The other brother, who was not present in the dayroom, said he was Hamilton from West-side Piru.

We talked for awhile. Then Peabody offered to let me read his court transcripts, indicating the charges brought against him. I guess he wanted me to see that he was a mega Blood. I didn't remember his face from YTS, but his name I later recalled. I couldn't read that well at all. But with my third grade reading ability I clearly grasped the understanding of his cases. One I read that he was charged with a gas-station murder and robbery.

And the other charge was a gang-murder. The transcripts read that he had drawn a casket on the sidewalk with spray-paint, and made a Crip lay in it and killed him as he lay down. We remained cellies for only a week. One afternoon Peabody was called for an unexpected visit. He quickly threw his clothes and belongings on his bunk.

I wasn't particularly interested in who Peabody went to his visit. He returned from his visit after about an hour. He looked on his bunk and aid, "Who took my fifty dollars?" As he fondled around searching his shirt pocket and other clothing he had thrown on his bunk. Nobody answered. Peabody then called down the tier to his Crip buddies, "Hey, Bosco!"

Bosco replied, "Yeah."

"Somebody stole my fifty dollars," Peabody said.

Bosco said, "I bet it was that cat-eyed nigga! We'll be down there tomorrow morning when they rack the gates for breakfast."

Peabody was silent all the night. By Peabody, Hamilton, and I being Bloods, I knew he didn't think Hamilton or me took his money. The morning arrived and the gates roared opened for chow release. Seven Crips mobbed in our cell and said, "Nobody leaves." After the seventh entered, the gate clinked shut. they mobbed around the cell trying to look hard and intimidate the cellies. I was slightly afraid, but I knew Wood-Rat from Compton Crips. he knew I was a reputable soldier.

I was sitting on my bunk, leaning back, with my left foot pressed up against the upper bars.

They ordered everyone to stand up and turn their pockets inside out. Everyone in the cell complied, except me. This big ass Crip named Ship, from Beach Street, looked at me with disgust and blurted, "What's wrong with you?" "Why you ain't up and turning your pockets inside out like everybody else?" "I don't have to turn nothing out! Peabody knows I ain't took no money," I said, as I stood and prepared to fight.

Ship saw that Wood-Rat and the other Crips weren't focusing on me, at all. Their gestures implied that he was on his own. Wood-Rat started hitting Hamilton with a whirlwind of blows. Hamilton started crying and shouting, "Tell them, Peabody! I didn't take the money! Tell them Peabody, tell them!" As he curled up his body trying to protect his face while this was transpiring, Bosco was choking the Cuban to the point that he defecated on himself.

Everybody who was suspected of taking the money was beaten, except me. I really felt for the homie, Hamilton. However, my heart wouldn't allow me to go up against seven Crips, and Peabody, with three of them holding knives. Wood-Rat was the only one beating on Hamilton. After they finished whipping on everybody, they sat in the cell taunting them. Finally, the gates racked open for lunch.

Everyone left the cell. Somehow the Cuban had put the money back on Peabody's bunk.

While walking to the chow-hall, the Cuban went behind a concealed window in the hallway with the police to point out the individuals who jumped him and the other cell mates.

The window was designed for such purposes. Peabody went to the hole with the seven Crips.

Hamilton and I were still cellies. He said he couldn't understand why Peabody allowed that ordeal to take place like it did. Hamilton said he was going to tell all of his homeboys about the shit Peabody did.

A few months went by and I heard from a source that a crime-partner of mine was in a module on the third floor. I roamed up to the third floor hoping to make contact with him. My endeavor was in vain. The police caught me and sent me to the hole for three days. I was charged with a roaming violation. When I was released from the hole, I was placed in a different module. The module was numbered 21-23 hundred.

I was a "freeway-sleeper." Since the Los Angeles County Jail was overcrowded. When this happens, the officials put about thirty bunks on the tier for prisoners to sleep on. They termed it, "freeway-sleepers." One day I put my iron knife in a cell that was used for the freeway-sleeper's bathroom. I went back to get it within a few minutes and it wasn't there. I saw a Mexican coming out, I figured he could have taken it and I asked him, if he took my knife? He acted as though he didn't understand English. I blurted to him, "You mutha fucka going to fuck around and start some shit!" That night around 9 P.M., all the freeway-sleepers went to the upper tier dayroom for the mandatory count.

As we waited for the deputy to come and do his count, I was sitting on a bench mounted to the wall.

Four Mexicans walked up to me aggressively. I quickly got up off the bench and to my feet and started fighting. Somehow I slipped and fell to my knees. My hands were on the ground.

They started tabbing me in the back. I glanced upward and saw the guy who I suspected took my knife holding it in his hand. Thank God he didn't use it, because I believe it would have done more serious damage than the others.

It was a metal slab of 1 ½ inches in width, 6 ½ inches in length, and razor sharp. He either froze in the heat of battle or spared me. Either one of them w3as fine with me. The deputies heard the commotion, but by the time they made their way to the dayroom, everyone had dispersed.

Consequently, the authorities didn't know who was involved. At that time, the only thing that was on my mind was vengeance.

But, within minutes I began to fell severe pain in my chest. It became very difficult to breathe. I was forced to tell the deputy that I had been hit. They escorted me to the medical department located on the first floor. The pain was now excruciating. I thought I was going to die.

The doctor was a tall light-complexioned black man, perhaps in his mid-50's. he had a very feminine aura about him. As he examined me while lying on my stomach with my shirt pulled up to my neck. The doctor was playing humorous games while I was dying!

He was making playful remarks as he touched my behind. "Where did they hit you at? Here?

Here? Or here?"

With his little silly giggles he touched me on the butt, each time he asked where they hit me at. I was thinking, "You damn fool, I'm dying, stop playing with me!" But I kept cool. I was in no position to be having a hostile physician taking care of me.

Finally, he took my pulse and realized the seriousness of my condition. Then they rushed me to the General Hospital via ambulance. According to the doctor, I had been stabbed nine times with an Ice-pick in the back that hit vital arteries connected to my heart. My left lung had collapsed. The doctor needed to cut the left side of my ribs open, to put a chest tube inside me. The tube would drain the blood from my punctured lung. The physician who would perform the surgery was an older white male, who seemed to be in his mid or late fifties. He was accompanied by a young-looking white female as his nursing assistant. I believe she could have been in her mid or late twenties. She was very pretty and nicely built. I wanted to be hardcore and not show any signs of pain of this death-threatening injury to impress her, as if I was some supernatural being. But shit! I couldn't control my painful emotions.

The doctor injected Novocain into the first layer of my flesh that numbed the outer portion of my skin. But for some medical purpose the inner layer wasn't affected by the drugs at all. The surgeon cut the first layer of my flesh with a sharp metal object. He then ripped through the other layer of my meat with the dull edge of what seemed to have been preschool scissors.

As he forced the medical instrument through me, I heard a gushing sound of wind coming from the hole he had just forced through my side. I had never experience that kind of pain in my entire life. I began to groan loudly, "Oh, God! Help me! Please help me!" I reiterated these words for perhaps one minute.

Trying to impress the pretty white girl became the last thing on my mind. At that point I didn't give a damn how she viewed my virility. Finally, after the surgery I was relieved. I was confined to the hospital fifth-floor where prisoners had a room that consisted of six beds.

My mother was informed that I had been in the hospital for a serious injury. She immediately came to visit me.

Thank God, I had gotten better by the time she arrived. No matter what I've done or been through, my mother never forsook me. Over the years she faithfully writes me and extends tokens of unconditional love. Of course, she disapproves of the lifestyle I chose to live. In her views, I should have been an evangelist. However, I knew from the beginning that it wasn't meant to be.

I remained in the hospital with tube inside me for sixteen days. The usual procedure for this type of injury would have required a three-day treatment. Being that some vital arteries were damaged, my treatment would require a sixteen-day over stay. Nevertheless, I made it through this ordeal and returned back to the county jail.

There was a gang-investigating-unit waiting to interview me. He showed me some pictures of perhaps twenty Mexicans. I recognized the attackers when he started flipping the pictures. He asked if I saw any of the guys who stabbed me.

I said, "No."

He then asked me, "Are you willing to press charges?"

I slightly laughed with a smile, and said, "Naw." That concluded our interview.

I was released and transferred to a different module. 47-48 hundred was a newly designed module from the other ones. This module was on the side of the jail we termed, "New-side." All of the modules numbere4d from the 20's to 30's hundreds we termed the old-side. The new modules cells and tiers were larger than the ones on the old-side, and the control-booth was stationed in front of all the cells, where the deputy could walk down the control-booth and see everything in the cells and tiers through the Plexiglas window. It was a week later when I saw a guy I knew from CYA Paso Robles, named Tiaras.

I went to his cell and spoke to him about my stabbing situation. I let him know I had just gotten out of the hospital. Even though I still had the stitches in my side, I asked him did he have a knife I could use so that I could get back at my assailant.

They were still in the same module. I didn't rat on them because I despised rats. Tiaras told me that he had a knife, but he wasn't going to let anyone use it. He said he would go with me to help me fight my attackers. Stubbornly I insisted that he let me use it. I wanted the complacency of doing it myself.

I attempted to take the knife away from him as he put it in his pocket. We started fighting. I wasn't as agile as I was before getting the stitches in my side. He was getting the best of me, backing me out of his cell, as we bombarded each other with continuous blows to the face. As I exited the cell onto the tier, my homie, and Claudie saw what was going on. He quickly grabbed Tiaras around his neck with his 22-inch arms and placed him in a choke-hold.

That allowed me to sock Tiaras in his face until his partner jumped in. then four other guys entered the melee that joined in to help us. Now it was six against two. Somehow me and the other guy interlocked and started throwing blows at one another.

I didn't know I was hit until I saw a plunge of blood drop from my face onto the ground. The crowd suddenly disbursed. Running downstairs to my cell, I looked into the mirror to examine myself. I took my fingers to spread my nose and it was vertically split in two, straight down the middle. Then I walked back on the tier to show my homie, Claudie. I spread my nose. And he said, "Damn! You better go and get some stitches." I walked up to the control-booth and told the deputy I busted my nose on the bars horse-playing. I showed him the injury and he called for back-up to come get me and escort me to the hospital.

I was transferred back to the hospital that I had just left a week ago. The doctor put ten stitches straight down the middle of my nose. After my brief treatment, I went back to the county jail that same day. Tiaras and his partner were still there; they didn't panic and ran to the police for shelter, even though they were outnumbered. I told Claudie I wanted to blast (stab) the fool who cut me. He said to wait until I got the stitches out. I procrastinated and before I got the stitches removed they both had left the module.

Therefore, regular county jail activities resumed.

I recall the first time I saw someone get their butt taken. It was about six of us in a cell on the upper tier just hanging out and clowning around. There was this young dweeb looking guy (to the gang culture). He was around 5'10" and, 180 pounds, light-skinned and appeared to be around nineteen years old. I had just turned nineteen, myself. Claudie started sex-playing with the young dude. He would grab at his legs as he was sitting on his top bunk with his legs dangling over the bottom bunk. Claudie would say to him persistently, "You been fucked before, huh? Come on, you can tell me!" Claudie kept playing with the guy for about fifteen minutes, grabbing and asking him that question. The guy was laughing and playing right along with him. Claudie continued, "Come on, you can tell me."

Finally, the guy blurted, "Yeah, my uncle did me when I was little." He was ignorant, and naïve to have admitted to his uncle's sickness and foul behavior. Claudie grabbed him from his bunk and said, "Well, you are going to give me some, too!"

He took him to the back of the cell and nailed him as they stood. Vertis was another big guy who held some 22-inch arms. He was from east-coast Crips, and was Claudie's close friend. Vertis had a large towel holding it as he covered the middle part of their bodies as Claudie nailed the dude. The guy didn't put up any resistance, nor did he display any painful emotions; he just stood there looking stupid.

When Claudie was done; he looked at me and said, "Do you want some, too, lil'homies?" He was looking out for what he believed to be my best interest. But I declined. I said, "No, I'm cool." I thought the act was disgusting.

The gates finally racked to exit the cell. Vertis took the guy to his cell, I guess for a private party that was four cells down from the cell we were all in. After being in there with the guy for about five minutes, a deputy unexpectedly went directly to Vertis's cell, and escorted Vertis and the victim out the cell. I assumed the victim was put in Protective Custody (PC). And Vertis went to the hole (confinement). But what I found to be utterly ridiculous, and ironic was Vertis only had eight days before he went home. He couldn't restrain his perverted lecherous desire for a few days. By no means do I disrespect my homie, Claudie or Vertis for their inappropriate conduct. I've just out-grown the self-hate and self-destruction that has been deliberately instilled into us as a weapon to keep us in thralldom by our own ignorance.

As I became more cognizant to the white supremacist that governs the country, it is evidence that the prison system is designed to punish and divest us of our morals and ethics, as opposed to the rehabilitation that is false portrayed to American Society.

If they had their way we would all be homosexuals, and that would be their solution to the population control.

When I speak in these terms, of course, I'm not referring to all of our public officials.

Clearly, I am talking about the malfeasances that are underhandedly deceiving the people for their own sly agendas.

I believe it is inhumane to sequent man from woman or vice versa—for so many years, or the rest of their lives. But we have to be strong and hold on to the morals that we have, and not succumb to the evil forces trying to obliterate our existence.

A couple of months later, I was charged with another roaming violation and sent to the hole.

After I completed my three-day confinement I was sent to 22-hundred. In this module I was assigned to the upper-tier that occupied four men to a cell. The new cell mates introduced themselves. The black guy said he was B. Dog, and the Mexican said he was Joker. I told them my name was Mike. We all got along with each other and in most cases there was mutual respect with cellies who were trying to make their living conditions as comfortable as possible. There was one empty bunk awaiting a new arrival to fill it. The next night around 8 P.M. they brought us another cellie, he was a white guy named Billy, who was twenty-two years old. We all embraced Billy as our new cellie without any bias whatsoever.

Billy and Joker resided in the same neighborhood, so they had geographical ties in common.

Hence they stayed up most of the night enjoying jovial conversation about their district and people whom they might have known.

Billy became so excited during his dialogue—he got reckless and made a Freudian slip that I'm sure he will remember for the rest of his life.

Trying to explain a location to Joker, Billy blurted in a rash voice, "That's where the nigga."

Before he could complete his sentence, he suddenly realized who he was in the cell with, and as quickly as his words ceased in mid-air, B. Dog stood to his feet. He exclaimed to Billy, "What were you going to say, white boy?"

Billy muttered something trying to defend himself, but B. Dog wasn't trying to hear no justification. He said, "Get your ass up! I'm going to give you something to remember a nigga for, for the rest of your life!" B. Dog took Billy to the rear of the cell and nailed him as he stood.

Billy didn't even put up a fight. The next day he was passed over to the next cell that was occupied by four Mexicans. They nailed him too, and he came back to the cell looking violated.

I didn't feel any sympathy for him, but with the maxim that I have now, I doubt if I would have let the rape transgression take place, or at the least I would have made attempts to suppress it. Nobody deserves that, regardless of their hate.

By now I had been slammed in the county jail for ten months. I had previously postponed trial a few times for no other reason but to put off going to prison. But trial was inevitable, so I decided to go forth and deal with whatever my fate would be.

My lawyer wasn't very enthused about taking my case to trial. My case to him was just another case-number. Rather I win or lose he would be content. He suggested that I plea-bargain with the District Attorney (DA). In a manipulating manner he said to me, "I can get you a twenty-five years old to life deal. I thought to myself,

"Sheeeit, that's no damn deal!" He then tried to deter me, and said, "if you go to trial, the DA is going to seek the death-penalty."

I said, "So, I still want to go to trial."

I knew for sure with those remarks he didn't have my best interest at heart. Even though I was extremely ignorant to the jurisprudential system. I knew the death-penalty was definitely remote. In America minorities just don't get the death-sentence for killing each other, unless it's some kind of unusual multi-murderous crime situation. The court set my trial date to begin in a month. The trial started as scheduled. The first witness for the district attorney (DA) was my co-defendant, Michael Hayes. He clearly denoted that I was the gunner and the inciter of the crime. Which in fact, had I never met him, I wouldn't have gotten so deeply involved with robberies. The second witness was my other co-defendant, Clyde Simmons. He corroborated Hayes' testimony with his story that I'm sure the DA coached them on very well.

The third witness was a guy who lived in my neighborhood named Rodney Jackson. He said he heard me asking for bullets at a liquor store the night before the murder. And saw me and the co-defendants running through his yard on the night of the crime. The fourth witness was Rodney's brother, "Robert "PeePee" Jackson."

He corroborated his brother's statement. The most ironic thing about me and the two of them was that I used to bully both of them and Rodney was twice my size. But it appeared that they had won in the end by helping the DA send me away indefinitely. The other DA's evidence was trivia. Both of my co-defendants were granted immunity immediately after I was convicted by the jury. The trial lasted for a week. I was found guilty by a jury of eleven white elderly males and females who were suburbanites, and one middle age black male who was also a suburbanite. They found me guilty in less than two hours. I went back to court in two weeks for sentencing. The judge sentenced me to life without the possibility of parole. Four years later, I would be called back to court to have my time modified to fifteen years to life, in which I have currently served, twice, in fact.

After the life without parole verdict, I went back to the county jail and thought, "Oh well, it's out of my control now. I have no other recourse to turn to so I just have to remain strong."

I had heard about all of the foul play that happened in prison, and I wasn't too eager to get there.

Clyde and Mike went home, but while Clyde was in the county he had transformed himself into a kitchen Crip, another stigma in the gang culture.

I didn't mean to kill anyone, but over the painful years of my imprisonment I have been suffering doubts of my actual pain in the crime of being the trigger-man.

I've been told by a few fellow prisoners who knew my co-defender, who's now deceased, that he had boasted to them about getting away with murder. He claimed to have been the trigger-man and didn't have any remorse or disgrace for working with the DA against me, because he was a Crip and I was a Blood. The only thing I remember is what my crimes told me days after the crime. Being in the drugged-out condition hindered me from vividly recalling my exact part in the crime.

Nevertheless, I chose my lifestyle at such a young gullible age, and I will deal with all the atrocities that comes with it. Though I am a firm believer of the Malcolm-X dictum, "There's no crime to have been criminal; it's a crime to remain a criminal."

I live my life by that principle. But under the depraved condition of my surroundings, it is very difficult to live a lawful life—when the vast majority of gang members and prison officials are lacking scruples.

Chapter 3

Consumed by the Most Vicious Beast

On January 13, 1981, I arrived at the Reception Center for the California Department of Corrections at Chino, California. This was a prison where convicts went to prepare for transfer to an institution to serve out their prison term. During my brief stay at this prison, I obtained the knowledge of what other convicts opinions' were about prison and what's transpiring throughout the prison system. I learned that DVI (Deuel Vocational Institution) prison was labeled by convicts the gladiator school, because mostly youngsters were there and they kept shit poppin (violence), all races. The Bloods and Crips were even gang banging against each other at this period. San Quentin and Folsom were considered more serious due to the convicts there were much older.

I appeared before my first (ICC) Institution Classification Committee, using the knowledge that I obtained about the prison. I decided to request that I serve my time at DVI Tracy. But the committee denied my request, and felt that it would be more appropriate to send me to San Quentin (SQ) because I had so much time to serve, (Life without possibility of parole). While at Chino awaiting my transfer to SQ, I wondered how San Quentin would be and what sort of drama I would face. I had no other recourse but to deal with it head on.

On February 19, 1981, Chino transferred my property. The CO (Correctional Officer) informed me that I am scheduled to go to SQ and the prison bus was due to pick us up at 2 A.M., and to be ready per scheduled time. The COs came and escorted about twenty of us to the prison bus. This big ass green ugly bus would occupy thirty-eight to forty prisoners. There were metal bars across every window to prevent any possible escapes. It was a seven hour ride, and it was tedious. We finally made it to our destination. The COs took us off the bus, had everyone to line up in a single file, and escorted us into (R&R) Receiving and Release. This was a normal procedure for incoming prisoners. The Chino officials placed us under the San Quentin official custody. I felt horrible, as though I was being consumed by the most vicious beast, and there was no way out, but DEATH.

The R&R (Receiving & Release) staff lined everyone up, and they lectured us with their bull-shit policies. Afterward we all stripped out asses naked while these idiots body searched us, looking all up people's rear ends. I thought to myself, "A person must have homosexual tendencies to enjoy a job such as this." After the search, our pictures were taken. Everyone was issued their appropriate linen laundry and a fish kit, that consists of a few items of cosmetics, papers and tobacco. After the R&R procedures, we were escorted to D-Section, a Security Housing Unit (SHU), and this building were huge.

I was placed in a cage on the third tier. San Quentin architectural design was that of a harsh image of the old prisons of bars. There were five tiers and they were extremely long. Each tier would occupy forty-eight to fifty-two cages. The cages were nine by seven feet. The bunks were maybe six by three feet long metal slab. The cages have metal toilets and dingy sinks at the rear.

Of course I was nervous entering such a ruthless place. I cleaned my cage. I took the state issued tobacco out of my fish kit and I rolled up a few cigarettes. The shit looked and tasted gruesome. I believed it was donated to the prison by some reject manufacture company but I was anxious and restless. In order to relax my mind, I smoked the whole pouch of that nasty shit. It enabled me to sleep in tranquility.

The next morning I woke up at 6 A.M. I observed a convict on the tier pushing a food cart and serving breakfast. About thirty minutes after eating my breakfast, I heard a sudden loud burst of rapid gun shots being fired. About fifteen rounds. I wasn't scared, a more suitable word to describe my feeling would be terrified. I thought to myself, "Shit, I'm not taking my ass out there with all of that violence going on."

My young mind had gotten temporarily weak on me. But once I regained my composure, and the reality sunk into my thoughts that I got life without the possibility of parole if anything, these bastards better be scared of me. I was the one who had to live here. I didn't have anything to lose while I was in this prison system; especially in San Quentin and Old Folsom that were the only two maximum security Level 4 prisons in the State of California.

During this period of time, killings were common amongst convicts and it happened to COs as well.

Convicts and COs were being stabbed on a regular basis.

Now-a-days, prison life is different. There are more informants who are crafty and skilled in managing the modern youngsters in prison today. These so call shot-callers; the ones who portray themselves to be righteous while they harbor rats. If they really look at it, the prison administrations are now the ones who regulate the so call convict affairs. As far as who stay on prison yards, who gets stabbed, etc. They work with the inmates who have a degree of influence on their homeboys, or the ability to manipulate others, to work against the ones who have a genuine desire to fight against injustice and oppression. They want us to be content with being treated less than human beings while they continue to strip us of our human rights and ethnicity.

When I first arrived at San Quentin my mind was still set in a gang-banging mode. I sincerely thought that all my drama would be against the Crips, being that my entire life struggle was Blood versus.

Crip. The only relations I've ever had with Crips were with my crime partner Mike who was really only a Crip because he lived in a Crip's neighborhood. He was affiliated by geography, not that he was an actual gang-banger. After a few days, the SQ staff called me to appear before the Institution Classification Committee (ICC). They reviewed my central file (prison record) to determine what kind of program that I am subject to. They noticed my incident with the Mexicans stabbing me in the Los Angeles County Jail so they decided to keep me in Security Housing Unit pending investigation.

However, before they could complete their probe, I was in the mix of violating rules that Kept me in SHU for other reasons.

The ICC cleared me for the yard program. I went out there flagging my bright red color. I was the only Blood, or red color on that entire yard. There were well over forty Crips on the yard. They were wearing their blue flags. There were also other brothers from across the state as well. I would estimate seventy brothers on this small concrete yard. The entire yard was staring at me in a manner of anticipating some sort of drama from me or the Crips. I saw Crips who were once my arch enemies while I was in youth authority and camps, but the atmosphere was calm and peaceful.

Ironically, the same Crips who were once my foes embraced me on a brotherly approach. I was surprised but at ease.

That day, I met a young brother my age. His name was Hustler Ron. He was also from L.A., but he was non-affiliated. Ron was a Ridah. He could have easily been a gang member if he desired, but he chose to stand on his own two feet. Ron was tall, maybe 6'2", 215 pounds and dark-skinned. He approached me with his road dog (close friend) Fast Black, who was a Crip from Rollin 60's. Black was short maybe 5'8" and 210 pounds. He also was dark-skinned. They admired the way I came to the yard representing Bloodism. They said I was the only Blood who came to the yard; being true to myself.

They informed me that other Bloods who had come to this section went to ICC, and then they would return and leave the section.

Black, Ron and I bonded. It was three of us who were road dogs now. I have to admit I really love those brothers. They embraced me and didn't care about the adversity that could have been my fate.

Black was the most influential brother on the yard, and now had me on his team, a young twenty-one-year-old trooper who was eager to display my soldier abilities. Black was about twenty-seven years old.

I guess it was then when I started volunteering to stab anybody who was said to be foul. But I learned quickly. Prison life in the maximum security wasn't about Blood versus. Crip though occasionally there's individual or group conflicts amongst the two. But for the most part it was all about underhanded deception in a more vicious manner.

It was fashionable in a sense, to obtain honor and respect from the masses, to compete for who has the most stabbings. It was like playing games and my goal was to be amongst the top contenders.

Black often had to tell me to be cool, and that I would get my opportunity to show my soldier abilities.

At this point, I had never stabbed anybody, only my homeboy in my neighborhood when I was twelve years old. And it was an accident, results of playing with a knife.

A few months had passed by. One morning Black was working on the first tier as an acting tier tender. He had the section CO unlock my cage (cell) so that I could help him clean the section. As I walked down the stairs to the first tier where Black was waiting for me, he was sitting on a bench smoking a cigarette. Not knowing that I would soon make my mark in prison, the stabbing I committed would be the first of many.

Black informed me that he had me pulled out my cage to help him stab the other two working tier tenders, Fred and Shotgun. Fred was a Black Guerrilla Family (BGF), a prison revolutionary organization that turns corrupt in the mid 90's. shotgun was a Harlem 30's Crip. Black indicated that they were both jail house rats. I was nervous; but willing to perform. I told Black to give me a puff of his cigarette so that I could calm my nerves.

He handed me the cigarette and said when Pretty Tony give the signal we were moving out.

Pretty Tony was a reputable Hoover Crip whom I later learn to like. He was the fifth tier tender. He had planned this assault with

Black before I had come out my cage. He was watching the gun tower for us.

Fred and Shotgun were in the back of the building. They were painting the faded wall. They had just finished painting the fence that we would jump over.

This gate, approximately twelve feet high separated us from them. Black took a quick but deep puff of his cigarette and said hastily, "Let's go." We ran up to the damp painted gate and jumped over it.

We vigorously attacked our prey, who was still painting. Black grabbed Shotgun, threw him to the ground and commenced to stabbing him. shotgun started hollering and shouting, "They're hitting me! They're hitting me!" Black was handling his business. By now, Fred was on the stairway. I reached through the stair rails and stabbed Fred in his ribs. Then I ran around the stairs to get closer to him. that's when he started running up to the fifth tier like he was a track star.

The COs finally heard Shotgun shouting. They sounded the alarm and came running into the section like a stampede. By this time me and Black had jumped back over the gate and grabbed some brooms. We started sweeping the floor as if we haven't a clue of what's happening.

Our sweat shirts and pants had the gate imprinted on them from the damp paint. The COs noticed Fred and Shotgun bleeding and took them to the prison infirmary. Black and I were placed back in our cage.

The three of us, Black, Ron and I shared cells next to each other, Ron being in the middle. It was obvious that me and Black were the assailants. It was only the four of us on the first tier.

But Shotgun confirmed that we indeed stabbed them and he put himself in (PC), Protective Custody.

On the contrary, Fred stayed in the section and pleaded his innocence. He honestly didn't know why he was hanging out with a rat (Shotgun), so he was going to be treated like he was one. But he was given a second chance. That incident insured Black and Ron that I was a young soldier being that I always talked about what I would do, so it strengthened our bond. Months had passed and Black and Ron had transferred to other prisons. Ron had gone to Old Folsom. He inquired about me to other convicts whom I later encountered. I didn't recall where Black went but over the years a couple of old convicts of my era in San Quentin said Black went crazy. I hope he's still living. Perhaps he's in a mental facility in the prison system somewhere. As far as the Crips are concerned, by this time I had established soldier status amongst the Crips and Bloods who were in the other sections in the prison, by being the only Blood on this Crip yard.

One peaceful afternoon I had an unpleasant encounter with a Correctional Officer named Clark.

He was a tall, skinny black man who had a gang member mentality. He used to tell everyone he used to be a Brim (a Blood neighborhood). Clark had a disrespectful attitude towards everyone: even his coworkers' didn't like him. One day Clark spoke some insulting words to me, for what his motive was, I have no idea other than trying to impress a couple of Crips who were present. I laughed at him as though his insult had no affect over me but inside I was filled with rage. I regained me composure from within.

A few days had passed by; Clark was escorting me from the afternoon yard in handcuffs.

He put me in my cage but the door wasn't locked. Clark didn't have a key so he had to wait for the other CO who was down the tier conducting his business of locking convicts in their cages. While me and Clark waited I decided to try and trick him into taking the handcuffs off me.

One thing I knew for sure was that Clark was a hot head and wasn't too bright. So, I said, "Hey Clark, you can take these cuffs off me. I'm not gonna come out there on you." Clark replied, "I'm not scared. The shit that happened a few days ago wasn't anything." This fool was so naïve that he took the handcuffs off me. That's when I made my move. I pushed the door open a bit. Then I grabbed his tie.

I attempted to pull him into my cage. He was so afraid, this fool hit me so hard on the side of my head and he nearly split my earlobe. I immediately let his tie go and forced the cage door completely open, making my way on the tier. Me and Clark were throwing blows toe-to-toe. It seemed as if all of the ghetto nigga-ness came out of Clark.

Suddenly, I felt a hell of a choke hold from behind me. Now the fight turned into a wrestling match. Another Correctional Officer ran over to help them. As I struggled, I turned my neck half way around. I noticed that it was a white female CO who had the choke hold on me. They subdued me. I was a bit embarrassed that a female put a choke holds on me that I couldn't get out of. But one thing for certain, I never underestimated the strength of a female again.

A few years later, I heard from other COs that Clark had been fired for bringing an unauthorized handgun on prison grounds.

After me and Clark's incident, I participated in a couple more stabbings that I actually gotten away with, and that's when the Crips started calling me Ridah Mike, which in Webster's term means warrior or a person who will battle in a situation regardless of his predicaments.

Twenty-three years later, I still carry that nickname. Later I met my first Blood while at San Quentin. His name was "Dickie Bird" from Bounty Hunter. He was from my geographical area, Watts.

Bird was twenty-six, five years older than I. I really liked him. I believe it's fair to say he had me under his wing even though I recognized early on that my courage far exceeded his.

I learned a few things from Bird, but one thing I despised about him was he had a sick homosexual desire to prey on youngsters. In prison term we call them booty bandits. I recall having a weaker homie who was a girly boy in term of his femininity, long hair and a soft demeanor. This Blood name was Steel Bill from 89 Swan.

When he first came to prison he was a Walnut, a Blood set that no longer exists. So, I assume he joined the nearest Blood neighborhood he knew about to keep the predators like Bird off him "literally."

Bird once told me how he had a desire to fuck Bill. I would often tell him we should be focusing on building the homies and not breaking them down. I enlightened Bill about Bird's sick and lustful feelings about him. He just stood looking vulnerable.

Once I engaged in a verbal altercation with this Correctional Officer named Cox, he was a tall white man. This imbecile used to serve the evening meals with sweat dripping from his face. Sweat that was capable of falling into my food. I asked him to have some consideration and take precautions over our food. He became offended about me instructing him how to do his job. I responded in the same insolent manner as he.

This disrespect carried on for about a week or so. He eventually had me moved to the first tier.

One day when I was on the yard, this dastard Cox went into my cage and engraved a knife imprint (groove) into the metal bunk to make it appear as though I was cutting the bunk to make a knife. He confiscated all of my property and gave me a rule violation report. It indicated that I was attempting to cut my bunk to manufacture a prison weapon. I was outraged with this unprofessional fool. I immediately sent a kite (note) to my neighbor whose name was Rashad a.k.a. Speedy, a reputable Crip from out of Carson, California. Speedy was also the first person to call me Ridah Mike. I asked him to make me a spear for the purpose of stabbing CO Cox. He agreed to support me, but being that this was a spare of the moment situation; he only had time to make me a small spear, approximately three feet. And then I waited for Cox to walk by my cage. Finally, he came strutting his homosexual looking ass by my cage in a taunting gesture as if saying, "yeah nigger, I did that."

I thrust the spear into his ribcage. He stumbled while making a frightful sound. Fortunately for him he caught his balance and commenced to run down the tier. I didn't get him good, so like Shaka Zulu I violently threw the spear sticking Cox in his arm. I immediately felt satisfaction.

Within minutes the COs came to my cage and pulled me up, and escorted me to (AC) Adjustment Center, the highest level of the (SHU) Security Housing Unit. The next level to AC would be SQ Death Row. I remained in AC for over a year. Once I completed my term, the AC officials allowed me to go back to the regular security housing units but not to where I had assaulted Cox. This incident occurred in 1982, San Quentin. I would encounter Cox again in 1993, but this time we were at Pelican Bay State Prison (SHU) and he was a Sergeant now. While he walked into a section while I was a tier tender, sweeping the tier, he was outraged. He immediately ordered his building COs to lock me in a cage, claiming that I manipulated staff to give me the tier tender job. And he put the word out on me to his staff that I had stabbed him in San Quentin (SQ). By now I had a color TV. One of Cox's COs searched my cell and found my TV speaker hooked up to play out loud, and that was a rule violation. It made Cox's day. He penalized me by making me send it home.

But at any rate back to SQ, during the period I had assaulted Cox, my mother had mailed me a black and white television. It had been in R&R (Receiving & Release). Everything that enters the prison will come and leave through R&R. My mother had told me she sent the TV off months ago. I wondered why I hadn't received it. I finally discovered that the R&R Sergeant whose name was Spears, this unprofessional negro was playing retributory games with my property because of what I had done to Correctional Officer Cox. He kept my TV in R&R for nine months; up until they were forced to give it to me. I went through every legal procedure possible to obtain my TV but it was to no avail. Spears continued to play underhanded games. The only appliance I had in my cage was my Realistic AM/PM 8Track Tape Player. I was tired of looking at these dingy prison cage walls. Especially when I had a TV in R&R that was being unjustly kept from me. I had already been punished for my assault on Cox, according to prison rules and it had no relation to my TV being kept.

When I arrived to the new building, there were two Bloods there who I was elated to see. One was Ford Dog from Lueders Park Piru. The other, Goldie from Inglewood Family Gangsta.

Goldie had only one operating arm. The other arm was completely paralyzed from the result of a twelve gauge shotgun injury. Goldie turned out to be an uncut coward and a rat. At any rate, he's unimportant at the moment, I'll get back to him later. My attention had been on some other dastards San Quentin staff.

They created a mess that needed to be addressed immediately. So, I got hold of some material and I made two knives and spears. I prepared them for usage. Then I sent a note to the homie Ford Dog. I asked him if he was going to support me against the police. He gave me his adamant support.

By means of fish line, me and Ford Dog conducted our business. I sent him the weapon. We didn't have any particular CO who we plotted to attack. It was first come, first victim. About 10 P.M. for what reason I don't know, but the (PA) Program Administrator, a top staff official was walking down the tier. He was dressed in personal attire. The PA was being escorted by two regular uniformed COs.

As soon as they reached my cage I thrust the spear into his side (ribcage). They all looked surprised, but not afraid or even panic. Obviously I didn't get him good. They continued to walk down the tier. Ford Dog was approximately five or six cells from me. When they walked in front of his cell, he thrust the PA in the stomach. His effort wasn't that effective either. Being that was the late hours, there weren't many COs in the prison. About 10 P.M. the prison is shut down and the only reason any convicts' cells are to be opened are in emergency situations. About 11 P.M., ten officials including Lieutenant and Sergeant come to our cages and handcuffed us, and escorted us to a building across the hall (B-Section). In Security Housing Unit no convict is to come out of his cage without handcuffs. In B-Section they put us in cages like dungeons. They were maybe the size of regular cages, nine by seven feet, with cement slab for the bunk, a metal toilet and sink that is connected together, and sink being on top. No window or view of anything, even if the door was open. When you first enter the cell there's a metal door, after that, bars. So if you were to get outside of the bars; you are still locked in the cage.

The lights were dim and gloomy. We stayed in these cages awaiting bed space for Adjustment Center.

One month after being barricaded, the administration sent me back to AC. Ford Dog was still there waiting for his available cage to open in AC within the ten days procedure, after going to any new building, Adjustment Center (UCC) Unit Classification Committee called me to attend. This committee usually consists of five to six staff officials. They commenced to verbally reprimand my actions. I just looked at them, slightly smiled, and told them why I took action. And I clearly denoted that the attacks would continue for as long as I'm being treated unjustly.

They seemed to disregard my reasoning and motive for the assault. However, I believe they took my threat seriously. At the conclusion of the meeting they cleared me for the (VG) Van Guards yard, a prison gang that was created at Tracy (DVI) Deuel Vocational Institution. Van Guards were factors in prison in the early 80's but no longer exists. I really liked their head commander. Their final fate was trying to take a war against the Black Guerilla Families, Bloods and Crips at the same time. Their members started to renounce VG and return to their roots from the streets. Bloods and Crips were a mass majority of them. On this yard there were four Bloods, me making five. There were thirteen VGs.

The VG's leader was named Money Mike. Before he became a VG he was an original Rolling 60's Crip. We were arch enemies in Paso Robles. I knew this idiot harbored ill will towards me, by his demeanor when he first saw me on the yard. I didn't particularly give a damn about him either. Before I got to the yard Goldie was one of the four Bloods there. He had been slandering me to the Van

Guards. I didn't take heed because I hadn't done anything foul to cause any one to bring harm to me.

Nevertheless, Money Mike saw an opportunity to impose me; due to that deformed ass nigga lies.

So Money Mike ordered two Van Guards to hit me, a former Blood named Duck from Lueders Park Piru, and Easy, he was not affiliated before joining the VGs, but he lived in a Blood neighborhood. I never saw the plot. Duck called me across the yard to talk to me away from everyone. While he captured my attention, Easy was creeping up behind.

Duck said, "Blood, why have you been talking about us Van Guards?"

I replied in confusion and rage. I said, "I haven't been talkin' about no damn body."

Suddenly I felt a hard blow to my back. I immediately turned around and commenced to socking Easy in his face. He panicked and ran to the side of the yard. And he stood against the concrete wall. I turned back to Duck and started socking him in his face. He didn't get a chance to use the knife he had in his hand. In fact he never swung at me. I thought about Easy trying to stab me and I ran over to him, and began socking him some more in his face. He curled up as though to protect his face. To be honest with myself, I believe that the reason he curled up was to protect his face from the shotgun pellets that would soon come.

During this entire incident, the gunner, a black Correctional Officer named Miles, was shouting for us to get down on the ground. But by now I was too angry to stop. I continued to display my aggression until Miles shot his gun.

Indeed he did blast two rounds, hitting me in my lower body, knocking me to the ground, forcing me to comply. I barely had enough strength to walk in the small yard gate where they handcuffed us before opening the gate to get us off the yard. All of the other convicts on the yard were sitting on the ground observing the entire incident. I was handcuffed and put on a stretcher and wheeled to the prison infirmary. The medical staff informed me that I had more than two hundred pellets in my body but said most of them would fall out. I was treated and returned to my cage. After that ordeal, it was determined that Goldie was a rat. He had snitched on his crime partner, named Bill, who was a Van Guard. Bill later, came to Adjustment Center and he confirmed Goldie being a rat. By then Goldie had went to Protective Custody like the coward he was. He spoke those lies about me to the VG to keep the focus off his foul ass. I understand that he is dead. He was found dead in a car with his head bashed in. I also heard Money Mike is dead. To all young Bloods, Crips, and Ridahs in general, when a nigga is always gossiping about other brothers without facts maybe you should examine his file to see what he is hiding about himself. The doctor was right; my sheets had many blood stains and pellets lying in my bunk.

I wasn't permitted to go back to the yard with the Van Guards. I was in my cage without any yard to attend for over a month. One day I received a note from two of my Crip partners whom I gang-banged against in camps, Moe aka (also known as) Halisi from P.J. Watts Crip and Byron aka Ace from 52 Broadway Gangsta Crip. They informed me that I could come to the yard that they were on. But I declined their offer because there were only two other yards available for me, the Black Guerrilla Family yard and the non-affiliated, that was racially mixed. They were on this yard. But my concern was that their yard was considered a PC (Protective Custody) yard amongst the convicts. So I told Moe and Ace, the three of us can go to (UCC) Unit Classification Committee and make a request to go to the BGF yard. And if they tried to oppose us we would tear some shit up. They agreed but told me to give them a few days because they were going to stab some white guys who were child molesters, on their yard. A couple of days went by and I heard some firing sounds from the shotgun. They had accomplished their mission. So the three of us went to UCC as planned and we were cleared for the Black Guerrilla Family yard. I didn't like the BGFs. That's why I didn't go out to their yard in the first place. They claim to be a revolutionary group for the people but these niggas would kill a brotha quicker than a Ku Klux Klan would. They're always trying to dictate to niggas for their own personal gain. They never wanted a war with Bloods or Crips because of our numbers. But more importantly there were former Bloods and Crips part of their structure, which would always have love for their roots. But they would try guerrilla tactics to manipulate and intimidate us to keep us in check. They tried to recruit me several times. I said, "Hell naw. I rather stay a Blood and help build my own homies. I don't have to be a BGF to represent our peoples." Nevertheless, they embraced us on the yard. We remained on the yard and functioned according to their program. The four Bloods that were on the VG yard remained.

When other Bloods came over to Adjustment Center they came to the Black Guerilla Family yard, where I was. Within a month's period, five Bloods came to AC; Ford Dog had finally made it out of the dungeon cage, Crazy Dee from Campanella Park Piru, Seville Bloodline, Veno from 62 Brims, and Shamrock from Lueders Park Piru.

We all programmed according to Black Guerilla Family policies, but Crazy Dee had a rebellious attitude.

He didn't have no regard for BGF rules of any talking over the tiers or playing loud appliances after the 9 P.M. count, mandatory exercises, etc. One day a young Blood named Lil' Spud, from 80 Swan, came to Adjustment Center. Word was out that another Blood was here. So I told Askari, a BGF leader, it's a new Blood in the building. He looked at me with malice and said, "He not coming out here. Look at this shit," nodding his head, gesturing at Crazy Dee. It was already five Bloods and my two Crip partners. He didn't want to see us get any stronger. So I said, "Alright," and walked away. I called the Bloods and my two Crip partners together and I enlightened them to what Askari had said to me. I said to them, "If we allow these niggas to stop Spud from coming to this yard what kind of Bloods would we be?" I said, "Let's rush them." The homie Ford Dog said, "No, let's do it on the next yard so that we would have some knives." I said, "No, right now I got one." The seven of us mobbed over to them. They had already seen our plot beforehand. It was about fifteen of them. They all lined up in a single file military stance, with their feet planted firmly on the ground and both hands tightly balled up over their crouch.

The gunners were prepared to shoot as well, having their rifles cocked and loaded. As we advanced towards them, I had my knife in my hand behind my back. Askari wasn't on the yard. He went in first, when our plot was in process. Their leader, who was present, said to me, in a nervous and body shaking voice, "What's up brother?" I replied, "You know what's up." Crazy Dee picked up some weights, getting ready to throw at them. Ford Dog said, "Put those weights down Dee." So he did. Our attack became a stand-off. To be honest, I feel we were afraid and so were they. We were young Bloods who were just staying strong to our beliefs. We were ready to fight the BGFs, who were far more advanced in prison politics, military skilled, and organizational structure, but that didn't mean shit. We were young Bloods from Los Angeles. We demanded that they leave the yard first. And they did. It was the same yard they said Spud wasn't welcome to. After the incident, the AC administration made us a Blood yard.

My two Crip partners Moe and Ace came with us to the Blood yard.

It was then when the BGFs decided to label me a "trouble maker." I guess if loving what you stand for and representing it in a vigorous manner makes me a trouble maker, and then by all means bustas call me what you want. That experience with the Black Guerilla Family, I personally learned that it's a necessity to achieve diplomatic skills. But still I find it difficult oat indignant times to control my emotions and actions. I realized, by which the manner Akari tried to dictate to us, had we been more organized and strategically inclined, that incident could have resulted in a fatal outcome.

Consequently, we decided to implement some structure on our own Blood yard. We conferred amongst ourselves and decided in a consensus vote, that we would establish some mandatory programs to build ourselves.

Everything on the yard was advancing smoothly up until one morning on the yard, about 8 A.M. At this point there were nine of us on the yard. The homie June Bug from Fruit Town Brim had just come. And now Spud is out on the Blood yard with us. Everyone was called to assume an exercise position. Everyone was in formation except Shamrock and Crazy Dee. They decided it would be okay to stand up against a wall and converse in a felicitous manner, while everyone else prepared to exercise.

I walked over to them. In a harsh and insolent manner, I asked them if they were going to exercise. Shamrock replied, "No, I got a bad letter. My grandmother died." I thought to myself, shit nigga, if that's the case, why you out here acting like you're having a good time? And it damn sure didn't look like Dee was consoling him. I gazed at them and said, "The next time you don't exercise, bring your knife out to the yard with you." And I walked away and called the homies together, and I firmly stated, "Shamrock and Dee were in violation. And they were both going to get hit the next time we came to the yard." Ford Dog said in Dee's defense, "No, not Dee. This is his first time not exercising." So, I said, "Oh, well Shamrock is getting blasted and I'm going to do it the next time we come to the yard."

A couple of homies attempted to talk me out of doing it but my decision was rigid. But to be honest, I didn't want to do it. But I believe if a person says something out of anger, especially if it's justifiable, he should carry it out. Otherwise, he's just mouth and no action. Also, that's why it is wise to think before opening your big mouth n rage.

That night I made me a knife out of some iron. Two days later we were scheduled to go back to the yard. The plan was that everyone would be across the yard away from where the incident would be.

Free from shotgun pellets in the event the gunner fired shots. I wanted Dee with me. We were leaning against the basketball pole. Shamrock was maybe ten feet away from us operating the 8 Track Tape Player we had on the yard. I said to Dee, "When he bend over to click the tape player again I am going to run over there hit him in the back twice, and come back to you. You and me will walk across the yard.

He would probably be afraid to run up on the both of us." We were stationed directly in front of the gun tower. Getting away was not my concern but getting shot was. Shamrock went down to click the tape. I ran over there and hit him in the back twice. He shouted, as he hunched his back a bit, calling me a back stabber. I turned to walk away and Dee was across the yard out of harm's way, with the rest of the homies. Shamrock started to advance towards me, giving me no choice but to fight. Though I done what I set out to do, I put my fists up in a fighting stance and so did he. I said to him, "Come on mutha Fucka."

He was bleeding from his back. The gunner had been shouting for us to get down. I had thrown my knife between the yard's gate. Finally the gunner shot me in my lower body, knocking me down. Again I went through the same medical and other procedures as I did with Duck and Easy's ordeal.

A couple of weeks after this incident, Adjustment Center administration decided to close down our Blood yard in AC and send all the Bloods to D-Section that were Bloods' headquarter. Me and Crazy Dee later became arch-enemies. It wasn't related to the Shamrock incident. I'd rather not speak in detail because it was never documented. But me and Dee had an encounter thirteen years later, older and wiser. We reconciled our past differences. Dee was the most aggressive Blood in our San Quentin era.

Despite all the drama and lapse of time, I was still without my TV. Consequently, I decided to relinquish my wrath on the pigs. I got a hold of some prison material and made myself a zip-gun. I had everything I needed. Then I laid and waited for whichever pig who had the misfortune of passing by my cage.

After waiting for a victim for over an hour, a big heavy set black pig named Johnson came along.

I called him to my cage and asked him to light my cigarette. Just as he took his eyes off me for a split second, I aimed it at his face and discharged it. Johnson started yelling as he ran down the tier. I ruthlessly shouted at him, "Go get my fuckin' TV." The staff came to my cage. They handcuffed me and escorted me to the dungeon cage once again. But this time I was in Adjustment Center, where AC and B-Section were the only buildings at San Quentin that has these kinds of dungeon cages. Each building holding five of these cages each. These are the same dingy cages they kept the beloved brother, George Jackson in for many years.

Although we had had a previous conflict with the BGFs, the brother Askari told the police that if he saw one drop of African blood spilled from me, they were going to feel the wrath of the African community. He scared the shit out of them. They immediately released me from that cage and put me back into the normal cages. A few days later I got my TV.

I remained in San Quentin for a total of 4 ½ years. During these years, these are the Bloods and Crips who were slain—deaths in general would be alarming when compared to the modern prison lifestyle.

Pee-Wee, I don't know his exact Crip set, but he became frustrated with prison life and simply hung himself. The police discovered him hanging from his cage vent with a blue flag tied around his head. And this coward was afraid to go inside the cage to unleash him. So he decided to go and get B.J., from Harlem 30's Crip, to go inside the cage and free him. But he was dead.

Then there was Slow Drag from Grape Street Watts Crip, whom I knew for most of my life. He was set up and killed in front of the pig's office. He had been stabbed and injured by shotgun pellets during a negotiating attempt to reconcile a racial disturbance. His assailant lost an eye from the shotgun pellets. This incident occurred in C-Section. I was in D-Section. I heard about eight rounds being fired; not knowing it was someone I knew being killed.

Then there was Weeble Wobble from 80 Swan. He was found injured on the yard. When the police are stupid ass came and put him on the stretcher, they dropped him. that could have been the fatal blow. Ironically, I heard that some imbecile said that I had something to do with his death. I found it to be preposterous. Hell, I wasn't even in that building. However, not long after Weeble Wobble's death, I received a letter from his brother, who was in the L.A. County Jail. He inquired about his brother's death.

I couldn't enlighten him on anything but I sent him my condolences.

Percy aka (also known as) Weusi Pasadena Denver Lane. He was shot and killed during a racial disturbance. He took his assailant's weapon and they both were killed by a black gunner in the tower.

And the homie Lil' Pete from 5 Duce Peublo Bishop was killed on the tier, his injuries consisted of stab wounds and shotgun wounds to his head. This was also during a racial disturbance.

Chapter 4

Taming the Beast

In mid 1985, San Quentin decided to transfer me to Old Folsom. One gloomy morning a Correctional Officer came to my cage and informed me to pack my belongings because, I would be leaving on the Folsom bus in a few hours. They came and gathered all the convicts who were scheduled to be transferred to Folsom. Approximately twenty prisoners embarked on the bus. The only person I knew or might say I knew of was a reputable Crip named B.J. from Harlem 30's. Back in the 70's and 80's he was amongst the Crip's biggest reputations. In 1985 at Old Folsom, the Crip's damn near killed B.J. on the Security Housing Unit (SHU) yard. He laid down (stop functioning) and he never was the same.

Once again I was on a long tedious journey. This trip was about a seven hour ride, and we made it to our destination at about 6 P.M. We finally arrived there, and I was tired as hell. All I wanted to do was get to a cage and sleep. This prison didn't seem foreign at all. It appeared that I was just in another unit in San Quentin SHU because the architectural design was identical.

Five high and long tiers and bars, nevertheless I was in a totally different prison. They took us off the prison bus and escorted us to a black top on the yard where they search and lectured new arrivals.

Their procedures were the same as San Quentin's, they issued our usual necessities, and then put us in our cages. I scrubbed the cage from floor to ceiling which I do every time I'm placed in a new cage, to make it clean.

I didn't know anybody so I didn't communicate with anyone over the tiers. I've never been one who quickly engages in friendly conversation or open myself up to people like most of these dudes would do. I realize that a lot of fools talk too much. I, on the other hand, would kick back and observe my situation and listen to other dudes conversations. By doing this you can learn their whole history without them acknowledging your presence. For ten days all I did was sit back without saying a word to anyone.

When I attended Folsom Security Housing Unit (SHU) Institution Classification Committee they expressed the usual static and expectations that I'd heard so many times before. They cleared me to go to the Blood yard. The following morning I went out to the yard. There were about fifteen bloods and maybe eight Vanguards on this yard. The former Vanguards top commander Four Deuce was out there who I liked from my early San Quentin era. Ness was amongst the fifteen Bloods, but he didn't remember me from Youth Training School (YTS), but I remembered him vividly because of the Beam incident in the dayroom and his percolative demeanor. I knew he was a solid Blood, but the most stalwart Blood on the yard was Four-Finger Dave from Bounty Hunter.

Dave had four nubs on his right hand as a result of being severely burned when he was a young child. Dave used his nubs better than most people could use their full limbs. He braided his own hair, lifted weights, played basketball, and was above average in fighting.

On this yard, knowing the caliber of Bloods, I anticipated future conflicts. I viewed them as opposing Bloods. I always expressed Blood unity amongst all Bloods, but I admit at times I can be impatient and arrogant in a brow-beating manner that often causes strife. It was my habit to indirectly send threatening messages to any opposing Bloods. It was me against basically the entire yard.

One day this big 20-inch armed, stupid ass Blood named Hurk, from Hoover family, a Blood set that no longer existed was manipulated into stabbing me. Some other coward Blood who had just come back from the L.A. County Jail found out I was on the yard and became terrified. Before this coward got cleared to come to the yard he tricked Hurk into hitting me, or might I say scratching me. I was doing some bar work with B.J. from Bounty Hunter. After I had completed a set I turned to walk away from the bars, this big ass dude stabbed me in the back of my neck extremely hard. I felt a sudden shock go through my body, but I immediately turned around and started fighting him.

We both were throwing blows, hitting each other in the face. Although he had his plastic knife in one hand, it didn't bother me, I would not cease the battle. It took five shots of the Mini 14 to subdue me.

I had always told them dudes that if they ever tried to move on me (stab), don't think it's going to be easy. In this era, the police were shooting and killing folks at random.

In that incident I was found to have a small wound to the right arm, chest, and back of my neck.

The injuries that I sustained were so minor it didn't even require a bandage. Some of these opposing Bloods were scared and ran to the police for shelter that prevented me from coming back to the yard. I sat in that cage for about six months without any yard program. It was stressing me out, but I had always been able to adapt to any situation. I suppose this was their (opposing Bloods) way of taming the beast, huh?

One day a prison bus came from Soledad State Prison, and I was elated to find out that five of the Bloods on the bus were my comrades. There was Papa-T from 52nd Pueblo Bishop, Rick Rock from 84th Swan, Day-Day from 62nd Brim, Lil' Dee from Skyline Piru, and H.B. hoe ass from West-side Piru. At this point, none o them had went to Institution Classification Committee to be cleared for the yard, but my beloved homie, Papa-T was in the cage next door to that fool Hurk who had hit me.

His note read: "Ridah Mike, you just get at me and let me know what time it is and it'll be handled."

I answered by saying, "When ICC approves y'all for the yard we are going to get the perpetrators." I stressed to him vigorously that the primary objective is to get me back on the yard so I can participate in the drama.

The next few days Papa-T and the four Bloods who came with him went to ICC. Three of them never made it to the Security Housing Unit yard; they were cleared for the mainline (general population) leaving only Papa-T and Little Dee in the SHU with me.

The following day Papa-T and Lil' Dee went to the yard. Papa-T conducted a meeting with the Bloods. Ness was like: Can we all just get along?—Way before Rodney King silly ass made the statement.

Papa-T replied, "I'm on the outside looking in (insinuating hell no)." He wasn't trying to hear anything Ness was saying. He wanted to know why his comrade Ridah Mike wasn't allowed on the yard.

Ness quickly responded in disgust, "That dude Ridah Mike is not coming back to this yard. He is a trouble maker. All he is going to do is start some more shit."

Papa-T didn't even comment; he had his mind already made up after hearing Ness's hostility and faltering opinions of me. When Papa-T and Lil' Dee came back to their cages that night, he sent me another kite to enlighten me on what had transpired on the yard.

Papa-T's message to me was: "All of these dudes are scared of you. They don't want you back on the yard. Make me two knives, me and Dee are going to pop them the next time we go the yard." I told him to make sure he got Ness because he was the main perpetrator who plotted on me. I made two flat plastic knives and sent them up to him by way of fish line.

The next morning Papa-T and Dee went to the yard. I was anxious and angry that I couldn't engage. The yard period was a three hour program and had just about ended. It was approximately twenty minutes left before yard recall. Suddenly, I heard two thundering shots being fired from the Mini 14. Papa-T and Dee had run into a group of four of the opposing Bloods, who were harboring Ness, stabbing Ness in the temple and facial area. All except one of the opposing Bloods panicked and ran in fear, fleeing from the danger, including Ness. Much credit to Mudbone from Anthens Park, he was the only one who stayed and fought like a man. These opposing Bloods were terrified and ratted out Papa-T and Lil' Dee to prevent them from coming back to the yard, just like they did me. It's common procedure to remove the victim from the yard. Clearly, Papa-T and Little Dee were the assailants.

Now at this point it's me, Papa-T, and Lil' Dee without any yard to attend. A few months later, the opposing Bloods that had the yard got into a conflict with the Bounty Hunter Bloods. The

Hunters were a little too much for them so they again ran to prison administration seeking assistance. The COs were head over heels with them constantly bothering them with problems, so they took the yard away from them and assigned it to the Bloodlines and Bounty Hunters, as well as incoming Bloods. Hence me, Papa-T and Dee were back on the yard.

Everything amongst the Blood society was progressing smoothly until one day the Vanguards and Bloods were enjoying a nice game of basketball. The teams were mixed; Vanguards and Bloods were on the same team. Rod Dog, a young Blood from 80 Swan and a Van Guard named U.T. were violently scuffling over the basketball. Dave made a comment to Rod Dog, "If you do me like that—I'm going to sock you in your mouth." Or something of that nature.

Rod Dog replied in a rage, "You're not going to do shit." They got into each others' face arguing. They were so close their noses were nearly touching. I saw at any time one of them was capable of throwing a punch. I walked over and got between them and played the mediator role. Dave went about his way across the yard and Rod Dog stated, "Blood, we are going to have to do something to these Hunters."

I said, "Blood, we already got too many problems amongst other Bloods. We really don't need to be fighting the Bounty Hunters."

During this period Dave was the only Hunter who had any verbal confrontations against Bloods on the yard. Rod Dog was a young twenty-one year old Ridah. When we met I immediately liked him and recognized that he was a strong youngster. I was twenty-six.

Papa-T instructed him to call me to the side and talk to me. He had heard so much bullshit about me from the haters and foul individuals. Rod Dog had a somewhat negative approach towards me, but Papa-T had influenced him that he couldn't believe everything he heard, and to judge me for himself.

Our first conversation he somewhat challenged me. He said, "Blood, the shit I heard about you, if I had not heard from Papa-T I wouldn't be fuckin' (associating) with you right now." I found his courage to be authentic because most dudes smiled in Ridah's face and then talked behind their backs. I knew that I could have whipped the little homie's ass, but I gazed into his eyes and started smiling at him and he started grinning. We became really close and I put him under my wing. I had his brother hit in San Quentin. He honestly looked me in the eyes and said, "Blood, I'm not saying this because dude is my brother, but when he gave them statements about Reno to the police, he was sloppy drunk." I believed him and from that day I stopped looking at Dog as being a malicious rat.

I understand Rod Dog has devoted his life to Islam. I wish him well and I'm sure he's genuinely committed, but most of these prison Muslims are hypocrites and are hiding under the religion. They are worse than the Bloods and Crips. they would preach that brother shit, and then when something racial transpired; they would use religion to cover up their cowardice.

A few days after Rod Dog and Dave's verbal dispute, Papa-T and Dave got into an argument.

Me, Papa-T, and a couple other homies were sitting at a yard table. Dave and a few Hunter homies were across the yard squatting. Dave and Papa-T argued from within twenty feet. I gestured a hand wave to Papa-T saying don't say nothing to him. Dave arrogantly stated to me, "Yeah, that's right, tell him to shut up." Then he said, "Fuck y'all, and this Bounty Hunter."

Papa-T said to me, "We are going to have to do something to these Bounty Hunters." I told him the same as I did Rod Dog. People called me a trouble maker, but I had done all I could to prevent unnecessary chaos amongst the homies. Dave had done something else that I can't recall, but by now I was pushed to my limit. I had the audacity to give Dave a kite to send along the way to another homie.

The kite was telling the homie to hit Dave. Dave opened the kite and read it. He realized that I had plotted to have him hit, and had the audacity to have him conspire against himself.

When the COs escorted us to the yard we could only wear our boxer shorts and shoes. The remaining clothes we had to put on once we were locked in the yard. Dave was on the yard before me on this cold breezy morning around 7:30. I was at a table getting dressed. I had my boxers on and one shoe and sock. As I attempted to put on my other sock. Dave walked over and rushed me like a raging bull, stabbing me in my right rib and immediately socking me upside my head with those nubs, knocking me back about four feet. He did it so smoothly I had no time to react, and I was half-naked. This incident happened directly in front of the gunner, approximately fifteen yards away. The gunner quickly put the yard down, so I stayed down and accepted the loss. The COs removed both of us off the yard and escorted me to the prison infirmary. They put a bandage over my wound that appeared to have penetrated my skin about half an inch, nothing serious. I never hated Dave, nor did I harbor any ill will. I got completely over it in about ten years. We were listed as documented enemies. In 1995, my desire was to get him off my enemy list, but the Pelican Bay State Prison (PBSP), Security Housing Unit counselor, D.

Ayala denied my request. Before I could get him off my enemy list in 1994, I was placed on C-Status mainline. The PBSP staff made an error and put me on the same yard. In fact, I was put in the same building with Dave. Me and Pookie had just got out of the SHU together and went to the same cage in General Population

(GP). During the evening meal we had to walk to the chow hall. As I walked in the line I saw Dave sitting at a four seat table with three other dudes. He noticed me as well, we made eye contact. I didn't anticipate seeing him. he didn't think I remembered him. Dave said, "You don't know who I am, huh?"

I said, "Yeah Dave."

He smiled and so did I. then as I walked down the chow line he said he was going to send me a kite. Later that night a tier tender brought me Dave's kite. It read, "That shit that happened a long time ago, you know you were wrong for the shit you do, but I'm not tripping (willing to reconcile). So I responded to him in reconciliation as well. It had been nine years, but what really disturbed me was some ignorant ass dude lied and told Dave that I told him to hit Dave, which was an absolute lie.

That would make me a coward to tell someone to hit a person who had hit me, when I was afforded the opportunity to do it myself. For one, I was reckless and wrong for attempting to have a homie hit Dave for an argument. I should have let them fight. Sometimes it's best to release your animosity. I stayed at Folsom for a year and a half.

In 1966, the California Department of Corrections (CDC) system started to open a new architectural designed prison. This new technology was created for a more confined and controlling method. Each time they constructed a more confined Security Housing Unit (SHU). I was amongst the first convicts who would be transferred to that institution.

On October 8, 1986 Folsom decided to transfer me to California Correctional Institute (CCI) Tehachapi State Prison Security Housing Unit (SHU). This architectural design was much different than San Quentin and Folsom. The outside of the buildings looked like warehouse compounds. Inside the buildings the gun tower (control booth) was stationed directly in front of the cages, the entire front being Plexiglas windows. There were only two tiers, and the cages were much bigger. The upper and lower bunks were metal slab, and welded to the concrete wall. The locker was on the opposite wall. Two of them consisted of four cabinets on each one. A metal desk and a seat were placed at the rear. The toilet and sink were by the door, which was operated by electrical devices from the tower. The air-vent outlet was connected to four cages, upper and lower tiers, and their neighbors. This allowed four-way communication through the air vent. There were three sections, which made it difficult to communicate with other prisoners in other sections.

So later that night when the CO walked the tiers for the 11 P.M. count, I approached the cage door and told the Correctional Officer that I stabbed my cellie and that he wanted to be removed from the cell.

I denoted that Bone wasn't responsible for what happened. The CO went to contact the facility lieutenant, who was a black man. The Lieutenant and medical staff came to our cage approximately thirty minutes later. I confirmed to the Lieutenant what I had said to the floor CO. They acted as though I wasn't serious and just playing games with them. So Bone came to the door to confirm my admission of stabbing him. the MTA examined Bone's injuries, none of them were serious. He had one on his arm and two more on his upper back area. They patched him up with a few large bandages.

The bitch ass Lieutenant told Bone that he couldn't move him that night. This animal didn't care if we killed each other or not. I wasn't going to give these animals the satisfaction, Bone was still a bit nervous. He hated me, but we slept in the cage that night in peace. After the incident I had flushed the knife down the toilet. The following morning the COs started conducting the morning showers. He finally made his way down to our cage to give us a shower in our section. We were both escorted to two separate showers, one on each side of the section. I took my shower, and then ten minutes later the CO came back to the section and escorted me back to my cage. The Correctional Officer then went to the other shower where Bone was, and asked if he was finished? Bone response was, "I'm not going back to that cell" and he was firm in his decision.

They called me to the nit office for questioning. I stuck with the story I had already told them for Bone's sake, so he wouldn't get a Rules Violation Report.

They separated us, and then took me out of my cage and put me in another section. Bone was placed back into that cage, but we remained on the same yard together. A couple of opposing San Quentin Black Guerrilla Family (BGF), who were here in Tehachapi with me saw an opportunity to disseminate some propaganda that I had tried to rape Bone. If I had tried, he would had been one scary or stupid nigga because he had ample opportunities to kill me, or seek vengeance. But rumors don't have validity to them, when so many people know certain people's character and being a booty bandit was not something I was known for. There wasn't anything feminine about Bone. Shit, had I been subject to such sickness he wouldn't have had to worry about me poking him.

I would tell them, you better be glad I'm not a booty bandit (A dude who preys on the weak for sex in prison). A lot of brothers oppose that kind of conduct, and I'm one of them. I can't stand when homosexuals come around me. Grown asses' men walking around shaking their butts and trying to act like they are females. This is a degrading image for the Black man. As far as rape is concerned, it doesn't really happen in prison as the public portrays it. That all men in prisons are demoralized animals (A myth). Those BGFs who opposed me have gotten weak over the years. They became informants and resided in Protective Custody, (PC). One, I heard had turned into a homosexual. These are the big bad principle functioning niggas who opposed a young Ridah in San Quentin. God has a unique way of protecting his righteous people.

Bone made it home on his expected date. I actually liked Blood and I still do. I wish him well and I truly regret getting into that predicament with him.

A few days after being caged by myself, the Correctional Officers moved a young Blood, Ridah in the cage with me. His name was Sleepy from Tree Top Piny. He was twenty-two years old. I was twenty-six. We stayed cellies for nine months.

The CO who worked our section was named Cole. Me and this fool used to have some serious insulting words towards each other. This hostility went on for weeks, and Cole had done some scandalous shit that the bastard Cox had done to me in San Quentin in 1981. It was like de-ja vu. Me and Sleepy came back from the yard and entered the cage and this bitch ass Cole had come into the cage and took my television and radio. His reason was, I had broken the seals in order to go into them, which was an absolute lie. Every time these coward asses COs get angry with someone they result to the dastardice games of playing with peoples belongings knowing they would get a violent and hostile reaction.

I looked at Sleepy and said, "Blood, fuck these dogs. They are going to feel my anger. I'm not going to let this bitch get away with this shit. We are going to make these cowards come in the cage and fight us. Are you with me?"

He said, "Yeah Blood, I'm with you."

I mixed some detergent and magic shave powder with hot water, and I hoped Cole would be the Correctional Officer who came to serve our evening dinner, but Cole didn't come. It was a Hispanic CO.

He came to the cage door and asked us did we want juice. I said yes and he opened the tray slot.

I stuck my cup out with the hot liquid, and tossed it on him. He was in pain and shocked. He shouted, "Mother-fucker!" Me and Sleepy laughed and started to plot on how we were going to deal with them when they came to get us. Sleepy said, "You should have let me do it, you didn't get him good." We knew they were coming back. Cole came and looked into the cage window and made some taunting remarks. He said, "we are coming in there."

"You be sure your bitch coward ass comes in first," I said to him.

Me and Sleepy put on all of our clothes. We made shields out of our mattresses, and flooded the cage floor with shampoo and water, so that when they came in, hopefully they would slip and fall which would give us the advantage. About twenty of them came in with plastic shields, block guns, and electric tazers. The Sergeant walked up the stairs to our cage door and asked, "Who is Sims?"

I said, "Me."

He looked at Sleepy, "Do you want to come out?" He asked, giving him an option, but for me it was out of the question.

Sleepy said, "No, that's my homeboy."

So the Sergeant left. We had our mattresses for shields up and ready to protect our bodies from the block gun. They finally came up the stairs. The Sergeant instructed the Control Tower to slightly open our door. He shot at us with the block gun, hitting the mattress.

He fired three shots. By now we couldn't see what was going on, and to put our heads above the mattress would be a hazard, risking getting shot in the face. This projectile discharged about six hard wooden blocks about the size of a cork off a champagne bottle.

They suddenly ran into our cage like a stampede of wild dogs. We fought them maybe about a minute before they were all on top of us. While under submission, lying on the ground soaking wet, this punk ass Sergeant Lara kept hitting me unnecessarily with his tazer. They dragged us down the metal stairs. After all of this they had the audacity to take us to the prison infirmary. However, I knew the results were going to be brutal, but my objective was as long as you impose injustice upon me, and we are going to fight regardless of the consequences. After that incident, I'd gotten into a few more incidents. By this time California Department of Corrections was completing a newly designed prison. The infamous Corcoran State Prison.

In 1989, I was transferred to Corcoran Security Housing Unit. When I arrived to this new prison it's architectural design was similar to Tehachapi, the only difference was the cage doors were a thick slab of metal with thousands of dime-sized holes, and cement bunks positioned next to each other. The lockers were underneath the bunks. When we completed the R&R procedures, they were putting convicts off the bus in cages together who they believed to be compatible with one another. They placed me and a brother named, Bichi Damu together. Bichi was Kumi (A group of brothers from Northern California who banded together to promote a common cause of geographical unity and race conscious brothers in general). Bichi was from San Francisco. We conversed a while with one another and we basically decided we were not compatible, mostly it was my opinion. So the next morning when breakfast was been served, I told this Latino Correctional Officer that me and my cellie weren't compatible and he needed to separate us, because I prefer to be celled with Bloods. This evil ass animal told me, "If ya'll want to separate I got to see some blood, lots of it." Insinuating the only way he was going to separate us is if we fought or killed one another. I responded in rage.

"You bitch ass dog! I'd rather kill one of you mutha-fuckas."

I looked at Bichi and said, "Fuck these dogs, we are going to remain cellies and kick it (to associate in harmony)." He agreed and said he had heard of me from Tehachapi. He then told me all the racial drama he was in at Tehachapi with the Southern Mexicans. All of the other prisons' SHUs I'd been to had a category yard system, but here in Corcoran it didn't matter what race or gang you represented, a person would attend yard according to what tier he was on.

Bichi and I went to Institution Classification Committee (ICC), they explained their shoot to kill policy for violence on the yard, and they cleared us for the yard. The next day we went to the yard.

There was only one other black on this yard, and he was a Blood from Fresno Village. His name was Money Mack 10, and he was a Ridah. There were a few Southern Mexicans (S-Mexicans) and Whites as well as Northern Mexicans (N-Mexicans), who at this point were being teamed up against by the S-Mexicans and Whites. So the N-Mexicans were basically up against the odds, but willing to stand firm to their beliefs. In this stage the Blacks and N-Mexicans had a strong alliance as well as the S-Mexicans and Whites. After being on this yard for about two weeks. I was conversing with an N-Mexican who was one of their leaders. Not that he had asked for our support, but the conversation was insinuating how could Blacks stand by and not support them under these circumstances. So I offered my support.

I told him I would let the Whites know that if they continued to engage with the S-Mexicans against the N-Mexicans, the Blacks were going to get involved. I enlightened the Whites, who were their influence, of our intentions, and they pulled out of the conflict.

I don't believe it was out of fear, but the sense of what was right, which are the codes we live by.

Eventually all of the N-Mexicans were removed from the yard.

At this point in time the entire yard was peaceful for months, and then one day Bichi was playing handball with an S-Mexican named Toker, who was our neighbor. He was in the back of Bichi while playing and punched him in the back of the head knocking him to the ground. The gun tower guard immediately cocked his gun and put the yard down. He didn't have to fire a shot because everyone complied with his instructions.

The COs called both of the participants off the yard, placing them back into their cages and resumed the yard program. Toker's cellie name was Joker. He nervously approached me and Money to explain the incident as he saw it. He said that it was between his cellie and my cellie, and it wasn't racial.

Money and I conversed and decided we'll talk to Bichi before we reacted. After yard I recall I went back to my cage, and there was Bichi looking confused. I asked him what was going on. He told me the only reason he could think of for Toker punching him was behind the incidents he had at Tehachapi with the S-Mexicans. I told him what Joker had told me.

So Bichi said he was going back out there in ten days when his confinement expired to seek vengeance on Toker. Bichi and Toker went back to the yard in ten days. The morning they were released on the yard me and Bichi were the first persons on the yard. I was looking forward to witnessing Bichi beat the shit out of Toker. In drama situations on the yard it is standard that convicts go to the rear of the yard so when the gun tower shoots it'll prevent the full velocity of its force. So Bichi headed to the back of the yard and stood against the wall. Toker was on his way to the yard by now. I got into a squatting position and leaned my back up against the side wall to prevent myself from being shot by the blocks. I've never known of the blocks killing anyone, but I heard of an incident where it knocked someone's eye out of its socket. I've seen it bust folks head open to the point where they were leaking blood.

The yard door opened. Toker stepped on the yard. As he was walking to the back of the yard he was still putting on his shoe. It was as though he didn't have a second to waste before getting his hands on Bichi. Toker continued to stalk toward Bichi's direction. I was thinking to myself, "Fool, get off the wall and get into your fighting stance." He was still pinned up against the wall. Toker got up to him and commenced to throwing blows. By now Bichi was forced to get off the wall, as Toker continued his attack. Now Bichi started to back pedal while Toker was throwing blows. The gunner was letting them fight. Bichi was back pedaling so fast with his hands up, and the only thing Toker was hitting were Bichi's hands.

He back pedaled around the yard twice, literally. Bichi looked up to the gunner and said, "Are you going to let this go on?" Finally, the gunner cocked his gun and told them to get down. We all got on the ground. While we were down, Bichi started talking shit to Toker, and the gunner.

"Well, let us up again." Bichi said to the gunner.

The gunner said, "You know the program, once the yard is down, it's over. I gave you your chance." Bichi continued to insult the gunner and Toker.

I was angry. "Shut the fuck up! You had your chance!" I said to Bichi. He put a lock on his lips. I gave Toker his respect by nodding my head at him. They put both of them back into their cage.

Bichi was sitting at the end of his bunk with his back against the wall, legs spreaded straight out, looking stupid. The first words that came out of his mouth was, "You are disappointed in me, huh?"

"Hell yeah, I'm disappointed in you. You let a Mexican run you around the yard," I said.

He responded with, "I wasn't running, I was dancing!"

I became belligerent. I said, "You are a mutha fuckin' lie, you was running!" I regained my composure.

Being that Bichi and Toker had two incidents with each other, it was required that the administration separate them. They sent Toker to another building. Bichi and I remained cellies. Even though Bichi faltered in a cowardice manner, I didn't throw him to the wolves. I told him I was going to send Joker a kite (note), being that he told me it was between the two of you. If Joker gave me any indication he was involved, I was going to take up the slack and fight Joker. Bichi told me not to send Joker anything because he was going to redeem himself by attacking Joker. I agreed with him. So in ten days it was on with Bichi and Joker.

Joker and the entire yard was out first, and then came Bichi and me. As soon as we stepped on the yard, Bichi walked straight up to Joker and started throwing blows, Joker dropped his head and started throwing blows with his head down, socking Bichi in the nose extremely hard and knocking Bichi to the ground. On that punch, the gunner fired one round of the block gun, forcing the yard to get down in a prone position.

Bichi's battle wounds consisted of two black eyes and a fractured nose. I knew his feelings because I had experienced the same injuries in Youth Authority. When I returned to the cage, this time I embraced him and told him that he had done good. At least he stood there and fought.

After that incident the administration decided to move Bichi to another block. Joker moved up to the second tier to cell up with his homeboy. Now at this point there were no Southern Mexicans on the first tier. A few Northern Mexicans had moved on the tier. There were about ten Crips on the second tier. One day, for no apparent reason an S-Mexican attacked a Crip. They told the Crip that it was a mistake. The same incident occurred with different people being involved. This same attack happened on four different occasions, and the S-Mexicans rendered the same excuse each time, and these dumb, scary ass Crips on the second tier accepted it. I was enraged, every time one of them walked by my cage I would say.

"Take your scary ass out to the yard and fight."

One day the administration staff decided they would rearrange the building, putting people in different sections and tiers. Now you had Bloods, Crips, Black Guerilla Families, Southern and Northern Mexicans and Whites balanced out on all the tiers. They moved an old BGF named Fela in a cage next door to me. I didn't know him personally, but during my early San Quentin years he was like a prison legend and I was honored to meet him. I'd heard how he once took a knife out of his butt during a Board of Prison Terms hearing and started stabbing the Board Council Members. So obviously I was attracted to his Ridah ability. He was forty-one now, and I was twenty-nine. On the other side of me they moved in a young Southern Mexican named Grumpy.

He and one of his homeboy were twenty-five years old. It appeared that Corcoran staff just couldn't see the brothers and Northern Mexicans on the yard programming in harmony.

The racial conflicts from the second tier and other sections had made its way down to the bottom tier. They brought me a new cellie from another building. His name was D. J. He was a Kumi. I believe he was from San Rafael. The way I bonded with D. J., geography didn't matter to me, that's why I don't have an exact recollection. He was sent from another unit because he was engaging in combat with the S-Mexicans on that yard. D.J. was a valiant brother. I explained to him the situation between the Blacks and S-Mexicans in our building. He aggressively indicated that I should let him go out to the yard first so that he could set the first example. The Corcoran staff had set up and planned these fights.

They would bet on them and play all sort of mischievous games with our lives. They would usually let a person from each race go to the yard for mutual combat. Sometimes they would let cellies go out and 100 fight as a pair. D.J. went out to the yard first and attacked an S-Mexican named Moska. According to D.J.'s enlightenment of the fight, it wasn't much of a fight: He said Moska didn't fight him back and he was back pedaling. After D.J.'s first incident on this yard they put him on walk alone status, which is you being on the yard alone. My S-Mexican neighbor, Grumpy, who I liked and respected, was a soldier and represented his cause zealously.

I once saw him fight a Northern Mexican and he could really fight. At that point the Blacks were involved, but when we finally got into the action, I told Grumpy that I was going to try to avoid fighting him.

"Mike, I'll fight anybody," he replied in confidence.

I said, "Alright then, I'm going to break your jaw."

"Yea, yea, right," he said.

Later that evening Fela called over to me and D.J.'s cage from the vent. He told us he was sending us a kite to read and pass down the tier to a Southern Mexican named Pin-head. The note read:

Pin-head, here is a list of the brothers who are not involved in the racial strife. Reading the note turned my stomach inside out. I was so disturbed, especially being that I had the utmost respect for this old dude. I sent the note back to him and told him to remove my name from the list because if any brother is in it, I'm in it as well. I called Fela to the vent and I commenced to telling him in an insolent manner filled with rage how I used to respect him, but now he was an old ass coward.

"You scary ass mutha fucka," I said.

He responded in his upset tone of voice, saying my full name, "Michael, I'll bust your heart."

"And I'll beat your old ass," I quickly replied.

We both regained our composure and reconciled matters, up until the next time he enraged me.

The next day we went to the yard. Fela peacefully walked up to a Southern Mexican who was on the yard by himself. Fela stuck out his hand for a handshake and said, "Hi, I'm Fela." The S-Mexican grabbed his hand and socked him in the jaw with his free hand, knocking Fela to the ground. Fela deeply scraped his knees on the concrete trying to avoid being kicked or stomped while he was on the ground. I felt for the old fool, but I also laughed at him inside. The gunner quickly put the yard down.

A few days after Fela's embarrassment, one morning my cage door was open to attend yard for a fight. I was the first person on the yard. I knew it would be Grumpy or his cellie coming out next, so I remembered what Grumpy had told me about he'll fight anybody.

I didn't go all the way to the back of the yard. I was approximately ten feet from the yard door talking to the gunner in a casual conversation. He knew what was about to happen. I had a small blue handball in my hand squeezing and fondling around with it, waiting for Grumpy or his cellie to come out.

I looked though the glass window on the yard door, and there was Grumpy on his way out. He came through the door dangling his hands at his side as though he was loosening up to kick my ass.

"You bitch," I said and threw the handball hitting him directly in the eye.

"Good shot," he said with a brief smile. Before Grumpy stepped onto the yard from the out of bounds mark, I was there right under the gun tower throwing blows at him. by now we both were hitting each other in the face. He was a few inches taller than I was, so he tried to use his height advantage by punching at me with his head bent backwards to prevent me from hitting him, or at least to take some of the impact off. I think I was hitting a little too hard for Grumpy, but I can't take anything away from his soldiership. By now the gun tower was manned by a female named Cortez. A few months prior, she killed the little homie Tookie Ru from Lueders Park Piru in a different block, so I was being cautious with this dame. She shot the block gun and yelled for us to get into the prone position. I backed off a few feet away from Grumpy and squatted down. Grumpy ran over and kicked me in the shoulder. I immediately got up and he backed off and got into a squatting position. He said to me, "I thought you were going to break my jaw."

I replied, "Shit Grumpy, I tried, look at your mouth." Blood was coming from his mouth. He was angry mixed with frustration. He said. "Mike, we don't have any problems with the Bloods. These guys are just using you. You see their lights weren't even on so they could come to the yard."

The medical staff examined us for injuries, and then we were escorted back to our cage. Money had gone home so I was the only

Blood in the building at that point, so you could say I represented the Bloods tribe well, wouldn't you?

Two weeks after Grumpy and my incident, I fought the S-Mexican that D.J. fought when I saw him goes to the yard one morning. I thought to myself, "This is going to be an easy fight. I'm going to beat his ass." When I got to the yard before they opened the door, I looked through the window and saw Moska pacing in the middle of the yard acting nonchalant, so I strolled over to him without any hesitation and commenced to throwing blows. I punched him in the jaw and he surprised me by immediately socking me back in my jaw. I wasn't expecting that. According to D.J.'s details, he wasn't supposed to fight back, plus I was much bigger than D.J. We both threw about ten punches each. The gun tower shot the block gun and yelled for us to get down. I kicked Moska in his groin really hard, and then I backed away from him and got into a squatting position. He was mad as hell. "Let's get back up," he said. I laughed at him and said, "No, I'm cool; I'll see you again in ten days. You know they will kill a nigga quick around here."

My final incident in Corcoran was the day they let me and two other brothers and a Northern Mexican to the yard first, and then Grumpy came out by himself. So I told the Brothers and N-Mexicans we should let the entire tier make it to the yard before we let off on each other. They agreed. So I let Grumpy know that we were going to wait until the last person came out before we got this melee underway.

After the tenth and final person came out, we all started fighting. The gunner fired six rounds to cease the battle, so we all stopped, not wanting to be shot. Nobody was seriously hurt, there were only a few superficial injuries. A few months after that incident I went to Institution Classification Committee and they informed me that they were putting me up for transfer to the newly, built Pelican Bay State Prison Security Housing Unit. A few weeks later the CO came to my cage and told me to pack my property because I would be going to Pelican Bay in the morning.

Chapter 5

Cage within a Cage

March 19, 1990, I was on the bus headed to Pelican Bay State Prison. It was a long and tedious ride. We arrived late that night about 11 P.M. They took us through the prison procedures required for the incoming new arrivals. They finally put us in our assigned cages. These cages were fresh and had never been occupied before. There was debris of dusty cement and other construction particles lying around the cages. I spent nearly two hours cleaning and scrubbing this cage. When I was done, I lay back on my bunk and went into some deep thoughts of why I had to live a horrible life such as this.

My conclusion was I had no clue why my life had been so harsh. But now I feel that God has a purpose for everyone, but it's their obligation to find it. Perhaps mine was to be the most infamous Blood to help the fight of troubled youths with my life story. But one thing I know for certain is I wouldn't live my life again for Bill Gates' money. It's not worth it. I have one regret in life and that is not having a second chance as an adult. I had just turned eighteen years old when this crime was committed. After I got done contemplating,

I got up from my bunk and started to observe my new environment. This prison was similar to Tehachapi and Corcoran, but different in its own unique, or might I say harsh way. There were two tiers, four cages on both tiers. That required sixteen prisoners per section. There were six of these sections in each building. The front of the cages wee that of a large metal slab with thousands of dime size holes. My best description would be to imagine a giant cheese grater with dime size holes, that's the whole front of the cage. We had no physical contact with no one other than our cellies. The yard was maybe fifteen by thirty feet in size. The four surrounding concrete walls only allowed a person to look up and see the sky. I can honestly say that Pelican Bay State Prison Security Housing Unit was the most secluded I'd ever been in. At this point the administration wasn't allowing double celling. We were only permitted to go to the yard by ourselves or without our cellies because there can only be one.

To be honest, in retrospect, this new confined prison was the best thing to happen to me, being that my aggressive and assaultive activities kept me caged within a cage for so many years. At this point I had been in Security Housing Unit for nine years and two months. Now this Pelican Bay State Prison limited my chances of violating rules. My only contact was with my cellies, and they were mostly Bloods and I don't fight Bloods unless they are foul, and those considered foul wouldn't ever consider being in the same cage with me.

It took a while, but they finally started giving us cellies. By then I preferred to be in the cage by myself, but the administration imposed cellies upon folks at random. I ran through most of my cellies during my six year stay at PBSP. During this time I got into only three cage fights in which I felt was exceptional considering my past aggressive conduct. I had somewhat learned how to control my indignation, so in 1992, I was celled up with a young Blood named Rico from Black P. Stone. The day I went to his cage he turned twenty-one years old. He proved to be a young Trooper who had been incarcerated since he was thirteen years old. Rico had done eight of those years in the Youth Authority system. I inquired as o why he was in the SHU because in my experience the administration would put any foul person in your cage, a rapist, informants, and cowards, it didn't matter and I had a very low tolerance for any one of the three. Rico let me read his incident report that brought him to PBSP. From what I read he broke a Correctional Officer's jaw for abusing his authority when searching his cage while he was in a Level-3 prison. These are the kind of young Bloods who I enjoyed meeting and bonding with because they were a reflection of what I was when I first entered the prison system. I had a lot of love for Rico and put him under my wings.

One day he decided he no longer wanted to be identified by his real name, so we came up with Solo. The young homie then told me there was another young Blood in the section next door to us, named Pookie from 84 Swans. Solo had the utmost respect and love for Pookie. He explained that he was in Youth Authority (YA) with Pookie and how he was a major factor in the gang world. And how he fought the Crips and made the other Bloods stand firm in their crusade.

Solo and I remained cellies for a few months then one day I mentioned to him how I wanted to meet this young Trooper, Pookie that he was talking about and considers initiating him like I did him. solo agreed with me, so we agreed that I would move over to Pookie's cage and Pookie's cellie would cell up with Solo. It took us a few days to transact the swap because most times the COs' be acting like assholes. Pookie was a twenty-two year old dark complexion brother. I embraced him immediately because I knew we would easily bond with one another in the' Blood crusade. He had an aggressive demeanor, but it was based upon Blood versus Crip, in which I have grown to defy. At this point I was now thirty-one year of age.

And swore on Blood that I would never war with the Crips under Blood versus Crip again, but I would war with anybody for a righteous and just cause. When Pookie and I first conversed I understood his young gang mentality because I had been there. As time went on, I could clearly recognize his leadership potentials, and enforcement abilities. He wasn't a dumb youngster as far as intellect was concerned.

He had served nine years in Youth Authority participating in gang activities and I knew my task was going to be difficult to transform his gang mentality into a more organized brotherhood approach.

Every other sentence he spoke was disrespectful toward Crips. He would also use words such as Bigarettes, Boffee, Bandy Bandy Bars, removing the C's from these words and replacing them with "B's." Something I also had done. The young gang mentality Crips would do the reverse, and would replace the B's with the C's.

Pookie once got so frustrated with me while we were talking about Blood and Crip affairs and past events. He became hostile and told me, "You act like an old crab." Crab is a derogatory term some unlearned Bloods call Crips. The reason I say unlearned is because when we call each other crabs and slobs we are only talking about ourselves. We are from the same origin.

I politely responded to his hated for Crips. I said, "Pookie, I'm thirty-one years old. I'm not into the gang life no more, and in reality none of us in these yards and in the SHU." I explained that any Blood or Crip portraying to be a gangbanger, believe me, he wouldn't be on the yard with his foes period.

And that I know who my true enemies are, and if a person can't recognize whose his enemies are under our conditions he's a stupid ass individual. I then told him that one day on these yards he may have to battle side by side with the same Crips in racial conflicts. Then I told him that we got it hard in these prisons, being black men: we are forced to war with the Mexicans, Whites, and the administrative staff despised us. In some cases we were trying to kill each other simply behind some silly shit.

He started to realize what I was saying to him was actual facts.

Pookie and I remained cellies for about three months before I was released to the mainline (yard). Pookie was soon to be scheduled for release to the yard, three weeks after me.

In 1993, I went to an orientation program that we must complete before we are allowed to integrate with the actual general population (yard). Then I was housed in a cage with my homeboy, Duke, from my neighborhood 92nd Street Bishops. Duke was twenty-eight years old. When a person is released from the Security Housing Unit, three month isolation is required. They termed this program C-Status (Control-Status). After being on C-Status for three weeks Pookie was released from the SHU.

They put him on the same tier that I was on, about eight-cages down from me and Duke.

When we arrived on the mainline, it was on lockdown due to the Southern Mexicans warring against the Blacks. Therefore, I never made it out my cage, other than to shower. The COs moved Pookie to another building. We often communicated by notes. He would give them to this stupid dude who worked in the kitchen to give to a brother who lived in my building in order to be delivered to me.

One day this idiot had the note lying blatantly on top of his desk in his cage in clear view for the COs to find it. When they went into his cage to search they found the note and concluded that Pookie was the author of the note describing a conspiracy to me. They charged me and Pookie with conspiracy to assault another inmate. With this incident we were back in the SHU for an eleven-month term. For this I was outraged. After we did our eleven-month term, they put us in a cage together. This time they placed us on a different mainline (A-Yard) but they had the same control status program. So we still hadn't made it to general population. But this time we made it to the C-Status concrete yard and dining hall. On this yard, Pookie and I were the only two Bloods, and there were six Crips and two non-affiliated brothers, and a lot of Southern Mexicans and Whites. Pookie understood that the knowledge I laid on him about the unification of our race was a necessity. Yet, if the Bloods and Crips were set tripping and a problem arose with an outside race, and then it would be me and him against the world. By now we had been in the C-Status program for two months.

Then one day I went to the canteen to shop, and while waiting in line there was an eighteen-year-old Blood from Sacramento who I was talking to through the gate, when a Crip I knew from the streets named Hard Time from P J Watts, (he was also in San Quentin with me in the early 80's,) he walked up, so we killed the conversation. Not that we were talking about anything that was of importance, but this stupid ass nigga, Hard Time got paranoid and thought I was telling the young Blood about his foul ass past. I didn't know they were good friends. Hard Time was once in protective custody while at San Quentin (SQ) in 1982, the result of a Mexican stabbing him while in protective custody, so he remained there. The Crips then hit him several times. Afterwards the Van Guards and Black Guerilla Family hit him while at SQ. I don't know what he had done, but it must have been serious. Hard Time then called himself telling the young Blood that he had some paper work on me, which indicated I was supposed to inform on somebody.

The young Blood told another Blood named S.K. That evening in the dining hall S.K. was walking out as he passed by me and Pookie's table he said, "Blood, this Crip on the yard named Hard Time said he got some paper work on you."

"Tell him to give it to you," I said.

S.K. said, "No, we're going to get him."

"No, no. I'll get at you and let you know what's happening," I said.

When Pookie and I went back to our cage and discussed the matter, I wasn't even worried about what that busta (a despised person) said. I had always been content with my prison life! Because I had never done a foul act, and I knew no one could say a negative word about me and still be real with himself. But I also knew that people were always going to hate Ridah. So I was nonchalant about Hard Time's false critique.

Pookie was highly upset, "Blood, are you going to let that dude play games with your life by lying on you?" he said, being persistent. By this time a few Crips that were on the mainline with Hard Time, who knew of me from San Quentin, had heard about Hard Time's remarks about me. They went and told him that he was playing games with the wrong person and that he better apologize to me.

A few days later, my comrade, Romeo was charged for stabbing Hard Time. And he allegedly got away, but Hard Time and a former Blood who is a well known informant named Smitty, told police Romeo and I were the conspirators, sending both of us to the Security Housing Unit (SHU).

Again, I never made it out of the C-Status program. Pookie's name didn't come up in this ordeal.

I, on the other hand, had to serve an eighteen month SHU term.

In mid 1996 my SHU termed had expired and for the first time I actually made it to general population. A prisoner had filed a law suit on the Pelican Bay State Prison C-Status program which proved to be unconstitutional. Therefore it was canceled by the court. At this stage in my prison life I had become the most infamous Blood throughout the California State Prison System especially the Level 4 maximum security prisons.

When I first got to Pelican Bay General Population (GP), I had been in the security housing unit for fifteen years straight. Being in GP was like paroling home. The yard was on lockdown. The Southern Mexicans and Blacks were engaging in conflict (war) on this yard. When a racial disturbance is underway, the administrating staff would put the race who was the aggressor on lockdown for perhaps a month or two, sometimes less than that. And the other races would resume with their prison activities.

When I entered the yard for the first time I was accompanied by my comrade, Crazy Dee from Campanella Park Piru, Devil from Fruit Town Piru and K.D. from West-side Piru, which was ironic to me because he had spent five years in Folsom Protective Custody yard. The result of being a stabbing victim of some Bloods. Now here his foul ass was out here misguiding the young Bloods. This dude was going out of his way to get in my good grace. When all of the Bloods who were foul, or just plain cowards heard Ridah Mike was out of Security Housing Unit they panicked and assumed that I had to start creating problems for the foul Bloods who were straight rats. Since I had just gotten out of Security Housing Unit for two conspiracy charges as I described earlier, I was very cautious and discreet in my conduct around these unstable ass dudes. I knew that the first opportunity these cowards got send me back to SHU, they would willingly tap dance their ass to the police with the necessary information. So I laid back and conducted myself accordingly.

The Black population on this yard was terrified of the Southern Mexicans because they were stabbing everything Black on this yard every single chance they got. Every one of the black collective groups were afraid, though there were individuals in general who were valiant brothers. But on a group level all of these niggas were pathetic. All of these Black groups, the Bloods, Crips, Kumi, Wrecking Crew and Black Guerilla Families were pointing the finger at the next group, trying to manipulate them to stand up and fight a war that was pertaining to us all. I couldn't understand how these niggas would portray the hardcore gangsta role and yet be afraid to fight. They were looking for any reason whatsoever to shun a war that was already in effect as far as the S-Mexicans were concerned. But when it came to Black versus Black, it was all good. They would be eager to fight their own kind. These are the same ruthless killers who were sabotaging and senselessly destroying our communities. But now in prison you don't have guns, it's about your own physical abilities and your heart. My intentions are not to slander the entire Black prison population. As I stated, there are some brothers who are genuinely engrossed with the love of our people and possess an abundance of courage. But in my experience in every prison environment I lived in, the dastards and foul dudes out-weighed the righteous ones. And in my opinion the dastards accounted for 70%. That's sad. And the only way they were going to stand up for themselves or the race is if they were forced by the 30%. But in most cases they did nothing but run to the administration and fabricated some false bullshit to get the vigorous brothers removed from the yard. Other races have their problems as well with cowards, rats, etc., but it's not my place to speak or worry about other people's plights unless it's pertaining to me.

About a month after observing my demeanor, the scary and foul Bloods had relaxed since I intentionally humbled myself to prevent any mishaps.

One night in the building I lived in, A-7 Block, I heard several shots being fired from within another section. The unit control booth (gun tower) had allegedly opened a S-Mexican cage door, allowing him the opportunity to come out of his cage with a razor blade to attack a defenseless brother who was a Kumi. The brother vigorously smashed his assailant, body slamming him head first, sending him into a coma. One thing I can say for certain is when you back brothers in a corner and force them to fight, "Dammit," we get busy.

The brother who fought the S-Mexican was my comrade A'Jene. Therefore he was very cordial about the incident. He expressed that it could have been any one of us. The following morning after the incident, the Bloods had a meeting about the matter. I wish that I can express the profound love that A'Jene displayed for the Bloods and his race, but it was beyond description.

However, my remarks at the end of our gathering was, "Fuck what the Crips, BGFs, and other Blacks do, we are Bloods. If a Young Generation (Gangsta) gets the opportunity to engage with a Southern Mexican and he don't, he is going to get beat down, and if the Old Generation (Gangsta) falters, he will be blasted (stabbed). There were maybe thirty Bloods who attended the meeting that morning and perhaps there were sixty of us who resided in A-Yard who weren't present. But the word got out and the jailhouse snitches were devastated. They ran to the administration, lying to get every strong Blood removed from the yard. A' Jene, Papa-T, and Ducky

Boy were baffled and removed from the yard. I found out later that someone was informing on me, too, in regards to this same incident, but I had enemies in every Level 4 maximum security prisons. So the administration couldn't send me anywhere.

I also addressed the administration ahead of time before I was placed on the yard, that there would be Bloods sending notes to them attempting to get me off the yard with fabricated stories, and that I wasn't responsible for what anyone wrote or said.

The snitches saw that it wasn't that easy to get me removed from the yard, so they secretly tried to spread a rumor that I was the perpetrator who was getting my own comrades removed from the yard.

When I learned of this gossip. I called a meeting amongst all of the Bloods who were present on the yard, maybe twenty. "I heard that some bitch ass coward nigga is running around saying I got my comrades off the yard. Whoever this bitch coward is, he needs to say it to my face like a man, and stop running around gossiping like high school hoes. Whoever it is, your momma is a bitch and you are a coward. We can duel knife to knife or however you want to do it, bitch!" I said like a raving lunatic. I carried on the verbal rampage for about ten minute and no one had the courage to stand forth or do something to me.

Finally, Sneak from Van Ness Gangsta grabbed me by my arm and said, "Let's go, Blood, before these niggas go and tell on you. I need you out here on this mainline with me." My intention was to force the dastards to come forth or falter like the cowards they were. So by them not representing themselves, if they said something else everyone would know they were cowards.

I found out later that one of the snitches was Ratcap from Fruit Town Brim. I will elaborate on him later. He was stabbed on a previous yard for being a rat. About two months later, me and two other Bloods were walking around the yard on the black top track when we encountered two Crip friends, Big Ant from Original Gangsta Grandee Compton Crips, and Militant Dee, I'm not sure what set he was from.

I knew Big Ant for many years from Youth Authority and Folsom. He is a reputable Crip, a Crip version 113 of my caliber with the Bloods. All of the foul Crips feared Big Ant. He was authentic and loved all solid Crips and his race. The five of us stopped at the top of the track in front of 1 block. We greeted each other and shared general conversation. Big Ant had an astute foresight. He suddenly said to me, "Mike, you notice the yard seems to be kind of strange today," I said yeah. But really I was just agreeing with Ant to be polite. Ant said, "Mike, I see white boys who are walking and conversing with each other, who normally don't associate with one another."

By now I'm really beginning to think Ant is paranoid. "All of the Whites are on our side of the yard and only two skinheads are on the other side of the yard. Here they come through the gate to our side of the yard," he said.

The two skinheads walked along the gate where it's common for all prisoners to hang out, for all sorts of purposes. When the two skinheads reached the middle of the crowd and launched an attack that was a signal for all of the whites whom already stationed themselves to follow suit. Approximately twenty-five Whites started attacking everything that was Black.

"Mike, they are taking off on the brothers," Ant said.

I replied, "Fuck that shit!"

"Let's go!" Ant said.

We immediately ran over to the warring area an estimated fifty yards from where we were standing. Me and Ant took one down,

Militant Dee tended to another. Just about every Black who was besetted fled for their life. Scary ass dudes. The gun tower shot their weapons maybe ten rounds to cease the battle.

The entire yard lay down in a prone position. Ant, Militant Dee, me and a few other brothers joked about the incident. We noticed that the two Bloods who were on the black top with us didn't come with us. Though one made a slight effort. We were in battle grounds and they were maybe forty yards in back of us. I didn't look down on them for faltering in that incident. Never did I say anything to them about it. I knew both of them were Ridahs, they just got caught up in a dilemma on a spur of the moment.

But Ant counseled them and they felt better about themselves.

The casualty results were superficial, all but one Crip was severely stabbed, and had to be sent to an outside hospital by helicopter for emergency medical treatment. The Black inmates all cried the same cowardice ass song of peace. Martin Luther King Jr. would have been proud of these Blacks. Not to mock our great leader and his philanthropy beliefs because he was a warrior in his crusade. He once fervently quoted, "If a person isn't willing to die for something, then he's not fit to live." You have to respect a man of that statute rather you agree with his philosophy or not.

The Whites went on lockdown for their attack on the Blacks for about three weeks. I got to give them their respect because they will attack if necessary, and then call for peace immediately after. When the administration allowed them off lockdown, in retaliation, about fifteen Crips decided to attack a group of three whites, one being a skinhead and inflicting the same pain on one of them sending him to an outside hospital by helicopter. As a result of the Crips attack on the Whites, the Blacks went on lockdown. We stayed on lockdown for about a month. The Crips negotiated a peace treaty with the

Whites, providing that all skinheads no longer be permitted on the yard. The Whites agreed with those Terms. By this time no peace treaty existed between the Southern Mexicans and Blacks. But one day the S-Mexicans were taken off lockdown. The morning they were allowed to go to the yard, they all went to their usual area of the yard and started playing handball. Basically, the way I saw it they were arrogant and didn't feel the need to inform the Blacks of a peace treaty. But there was one S-Mexican who was the stupidest person I'd ever seen in prison, or his courage was beyond any person I'd ever seen in my life.

While the S-Mexicans were secured amongst themselves, this one guy literally walked over 100 blocks. He walked through packs of brothers for maybe thirty minutes. Finally an old Black Guerilla Family and a young Blood attacked him and beat him senseless. The results of his stupidity made his people cut him severely. After these two incidents, the Blacks and S-Mexicans lived together on the yard without further conflicts.

By now the entire prison yard was functioning under the usual activities. No racial strife amongst anyone. It was good that we had a few months of tranquility. It was preferable to me; you see I'm not anti any race of people. My opinion is we all should concur for a common cause that affects us all. Since we are the o es who are forced to be imprisoned, let's make our lives a little more bearable, because the oppressors are the only force who will gain anything from our self destruction. They already have complete control over our physical being and in some cases, our minds. They will continue to create more oppressive rules and regulations to make our lives and time a living hell. In most cases the police stir up these racial conflicts to keep the focus off the evil things they do to keep us under control. But if I can prevent it, I will not stand by and allow a defenseless brother to be preyed upon without lending my emotional or physical support.

About six months later, another problem arrived in the Blood world. My stupid ass boy, Sneak, who worked in the prison laundry room got into a conversation with a Northern Mexican (N-Mexican).

This idiot told the N-Mexican that another Blood named Maurice from Anthens Park had said if he didn't pay that he was going to get hands put on him (beat up). Clearly insinuating that the homie Maurice was preparing to do something to him if necessary, this basically left Maurice vulnerable by him not knowing what was going on. This young N-Mexican was their leader on that yard. He and Sneak knew each other from the streets. That morning when I made it to the yard, several Bloods asked if I had heard what Sneak had done. They seemed upset about his actions because it could have resulted in a racial conflict with the N-Mexicans, if they would have reacted and decided to attack Maurice or the Bloods collectively. The alliance with the Blacks and N-Mexicans, and S-Mexicans and Whites I described at Corcoran no longer existed at this point.

But the N-Mexican, whom Sneak was talking to informed the Bloods about the statement Sneak had made. So me and a couple of other Bloods decided to give Sneak the benefit of the doubt, and discipline him for his actions by making him do exercises and run laps around the track. I told Sneak that in the future to leave that northern Mexican alone! I explained to him that the dude didn't care about him when he tried to cross him up. Sneak agreed and told me that he was not going to fuck with that dude again.

About three weeks later, I came to the yard when several Bloods approached me again about Sneak's conduct, and asked had I heard about what Sneak had done this time? I said no. it seemed that he had gotten himself into another predicament with the same northern Mexican. I figured that if he had that much contempt for the guy, and then why not just beat the fool's ass, instead of playing the stupid ass word games with him. if he had, I would have supported him to the utmost degree, regardless of any repercussions. But this dummy wanted to continue to war with words having himself and the homies vulnerable for an ambush if the N-Mexicans had decided to move collectively. Many Bloods expressed ill will about Sneak's blabber mouth conducts with the N-Mexican. I personally didn't want to see anything happen to him because I had put him under my wings, but when you function by principles and common law, everyone is subject to its guidelines. I told Sneak once before I wouldn't allow the homies to stab him for the stupid shit he is doing, but I would let them beat his ass if it was justifiable.

So I let another Blood make the call on Sneak. And he decided Sneak had already gotten the benefits of doubt when he ran laps and exercised prior to this incident.

Sneak was beaten up. The same young Blood that was talking to Hard Time knocked Sneak to the ground and commenced to kicking his ass. I really felt bad for him, but sometimes this is the only method people understand, and I still half-ass like the fool.

Now the guy I commented about earlier in this dialogue, Ratcap, some homies stabbed him on another yard in Pelican Bay. The result of that stabbing landed him on this present yard. After being stabbed by the group that he thought loved him, it destroyed the principles and code by which we live. So he became an informant. He knew that many homies were out to get him, so he started seeking all the support he could get. So he let this other guy who disapproved of Sneak's ass kicking manipulate him into going up against me on his behalf. Approximately twenty minutes after Sneak had gotten beaten up, the CO called for yard recall. All of the prisoners were walking back to their building when I got to my building A-3. Approximately fifty convicts stood in front of the building waiting for their section to be called, so that they could go to their cages. My section was called. About four Bloods were standing by.

As I walked by them I gave each one of them a hand daps of salute. When I got up to Ratcap he socked me extremely hard on my right jaw. But the instincts, God had blessed me with, enabled me to turn around and immediately start to fight. He punched me directly in front of the COs about eight of them. I guess he was hoping the COs would break the fight up immediately because he had the opportunity to do this way before yard recall, and away from the COs. But boy was he wrong. We went blow for blow, throwing many punches. This fool was socking me real hard and he had a height advantage so he was making a greater impact with his punches. But I thought to myself, as hard as this fool hit me I'm going to hit him harder. Ratcap fucked up when he attempted to grab me, by putting his hands on my shoulders.

I hit that fool with about seven consecutive inside blows that I knocked him to his knees. I was so angry that a rat had the audacity to stand up against me, so I went down to the ground where he was, to finish punishing him. As I punched him while he was on all fours knocking him on his back, I climbed on him and sat on his stomach while I was swinging these knuckles at him. By now his cellie, a Blood named Twin from Lime Hood Piru ran over and started socking me up side my head. I let him have that because he just gave me a greater incentive to focus on Ratcap. I continued to punch down on him in a vigorous way, hitting him and the cement ground knocking skin from my knuckles. The COs had to mace me, and literally grab me around the neck and pull me off that fool.

After the incident, the administrative staff was going to let all of us back on the yard together because a fist fight doesn't require a SHU term. But these dudes were so terrified they didn't want to see me back on that yard. They ran to administration with information that they knew would keep me from returning to that yard. So the police were forced to send me to the hole, Administrative Segregation (Ad-Seg). I was there for three days before I went to ICC. The committee explained to me that I wasn't there for the fight, and they were going to investigate the matter of me trying to start a race war.

The Captain made it clear that if the findings in the investigation is valid he was going to send me back to the SHU for an indeterminate period. But if it's determined to be false then he was going to transfer me to another prison.

In two months the (IGI) Institutional Gang Investigation was concluded and the evidence was insufficient to send me back to the SHU, so the appropriate method was to transfer me to another prison as the Captain informed me prior to the investigation. But the problem at hand was, I had documented enemies in every California Level 4 one hundred eighty-designed maximum security prisons. Therefore I would remain in Ad-Seg. pending appropriate transfer placement. After being in Ad-Seg for three months, I received word that my comrade, the infamous Big Bow Low from Bel Haven N.G. Bounty Hunter had gotten out of the SHU in Pelican Bay. He had gone to the same yard that I had my incident on. He stayed on that yard two days before; the informants panicked and ran to the administration for shelter. A chosen few homies finally decided to muster up their conscience to act.

Both Ratcap and Twin whom I fought were severely beaten on the yard. I commend Ko-Jack from Blood Stone Villain, Tu-Tu from

Oak Park Piru, Sekou from Bounty Hunter Watts, Willie Dynamite from Oak Park Bloods and Troy from Oak Park Bloods.

Four years later, I encountered Twin and he expressed regret for being at odds with me for supporting someone who he didn't know was a rat. He told me that after he was beaten, TuTu and Ko-Jack told him he should not have jumped in me and Ratcap's fight. After that painful experience for him, he renounced all his ties with the Bloods and started functioning with his race, the Samoans.

Finally, after being in Ad-Seg. for seven months ICC denoted the documented enemy I had at New Folsom was no longer in that institution, so they put me up for transfer to New Folsom. A month later the CO came to my cage and told me to pack my property because I was on the bus list to go to Folsom that morning at 3 A.M.

We were on the bus headed to our destination and arrived at Folsom that night. I went through the familiar orientation program that I am so inclined with, since I've been through this for over 20 years.

They put me in the cage with a brother named Brown, whom I was in San Quentin with sixteen years ago.

He had been home several times trying to get his life together. We stayed up all that night talking about past and present occurrences that had been going on in our lives, and how prison has changed since our San Quentin (SQ) days.

The next morning after breakfast, a black tier tender came in the section to clean up. He inquired as to where we were from. He said he was from Oakland and his name was Faheem. I told him that I am a Blood out of Los Angeles and my cellie is nonaffiliated. Faheem informed me that I had a homeboy who was a tier tender and that he would direct him to me.

Ten minutes later, a young twenty-four year old Blood named Lunatik from Pasadena Denver Lane approached my cage door and introduced himself. He asked where was I from. I replied my name is Ramani and I'm from 9 Deuce Bishop. I didn't want to reveal my infamous name Ridah Mike to him because I knew if the foul individuals found out I was there they would surely panic like they did everywhere I went in the prison system.

Lunatic asked me if I went by another name, I said no. he asked if I was hooked up (meaning prison politics). I told him, "Yeah, I'm a Blood."

"No, I mean, are you hooked up?" he asked.

Again I said, "Yeah, I'm a Blood." I knew what he was referring to, but I just played mind games with the young homie. He left to go get me a fish kit of necessities that consisted of cosmetics. 'Tik then said that he was going to the yard in the morning. He said that I had two homeboys on the yard named Ace from 9 Deuce Bishop, and Run Run from 5 Deuce Pueblo Bishop and that if I had a kite (note) for them, he could take it to them for me. I told him no and just extend my regards to them and let them know I'd talk to them when Institution Classification Committee (ICC) cleared me for the yard.

'Tik came back from the yard the next day and told me the homies said they didn't know any Ramani, so I finally told him that Ramani is my Swahili name and I didn't tell him my name was Ridah Mike because a lot of Bloods who hear that I am amongst their environment often got scared and ran to the police to prevent me from coming to the yard.

When I told young Lunatik my name I saw a bit of surprise on his face. He said, Yea, when I told them Ramani from 9 Deuce Bishop was in orientation, somebody said that's Ridah Mike." 'Tik had described me to them. Also, I am the oldest active 9 Deuce Bishop who's in the California Prison System.

'Tik told me that if I desired he could keep my identity concealed. "No, fuck it. They assume it's me anyway. I'll have a couple of kites prepared to take to a couple of homies on the yard tomorrow,"

I said. 'Tik said all right and he'd be back over to get them tomorrow before he went to the yard. He came and got the kites and I verified who I was.

The orientation section is a secluded building in order for the new arrivals to keep away from the general population. An inmate would have special privileges to come into the section and talk to the new arrivals. However, the yard captain granted the homie, Slaughter from 89 Family Swan the opportunity to come and speak to me. Slaughter was escorted by a white female Correctional Officer. He was accompanied by two other Bloods. I believe it was about 8 P.M. I didn't know him personally, but he was in San Quentin for ten days before I was called for, so I could get cleared for the yard. When I was in front of the Institution Classification Committee they determined that I had confidential enemies on the C-Facility, and therefore they elected to send me to B-Facility.

Young Lunatik came into the section and I told them where they were going to send me. He looked at me with disappointment. "I knew some shit like this was going to happen. Too many people (Bloods) were asking me questions about you. They were asking him how I look, what I was talking to him about." As though they were trying to figure out what I might do had I made it to the yard.

Three days after I had gone to ICC, I went to B-Facility. When I got to their orientation building, a couple of my comrades snuck into the section to embrace me. After a few days I was cleared to go to the yard, I asked some brother on the yard where were all the Bloods hanging out at. He pointed to a handball court and said over in Blood Alley, a term that Bloods named their area.

I walked over there and embraced a few homies, they acted nonchalant, or as if they had never heard of my name. little did I know these niggas had panicked too when I was in this yard's orientation.

That day on the yard I just walked a few laps and observed my new environment. A few days later while walking back to our buildings during yard recall, I met a young twenty-one year old homie named Sick Mike from Black P. Stone and seventeen year old Laniak. They both were some young strong and intelligent Bloods. So I introduced myself to them and I explained my philosophy of Bloodism to them.

And they agreed to the principles that I unfolded. Then the young homie, Sick Mike told me when I was in orientation how all of these Bloods were talking about me and when I came to the yard nobody did nothing to me. So he said he thought to himself that Ridah Mike must be a Ridah. There were a few of my so called comrades on the yard. Each one of them appeared to be misfits.

Having no genuine courage, alcoholics amongst other defile characteristics. After pondering what the young homie had enlightened me on, I saw why these misfits didn't want me on this yard with them. I can honestly say, all while my presence existed on that yard those dudes were sober and intact.

They hated the fact that they couldn't escape the reality of being incarcerated. A weak minded person would do anything possible to shun his troubled conditions, instead of trying to make his life or conditions better, he runs from the challenge. To me that's a coward. All along they were desperately plotting to get me off the yard without their scary asses making any sacrifices themselves to confront me.

While on this B-Yard many Bloods told me they knew I wasn't going to make it out to C-Yard from orientation, after I had told them where I had come from. They indicated that the Blood I had just met over in C-Yard orientation named Rat-heem was a big time informant and he had literally had over fifty reputable Bloods removed from that facility. Some of them made it to the yard and some of them never made it out of orientation like I didn't. I've never been the type of person to succumb to peer pressure, or function as a demagogue. Prison life is dirty; people will try to manipulate you to hate their enemies for their own personal benefits. Therefore I wasn't too hasty to oppose Rat-heem. I stayed on the B-Yard for four months.

An ugly looking little guy with all of his front teeth knocked out named Money was a Blood on the yard. Money was a Five-Deuce Peublo Bishop. There was another Five-Deuce Peublo Bishop on the yard, a hater named Red. When I first met Red, he embraced me, and informed me that Money was a solid homie, but he used to be a Crip and is a jailhouse Prison Blood from San Francisco. I explained to Red that geography didn't mean nothing to me, as long as Money represented Bishop right, he got my support. Most dudes who are not genuine Bloods and Crips are dangerous, because they'd do anything to prove themselves. They'd stab you and get lucky and kill you, not knowing what they were doing just to impress other people.

A few months later, a rumor was circulating on the yard that Money used to be a Crip. Money was my neighbor. One afternoon he came to my cage door and asked me did I hear about the rumor that he used to be a Crip. I said, "Yeah, Red told me." I didn't think it was a big deal. So Money asked Red, and Red's coward ass denied that he told me that Money used to be a Crip. Now this really gave the misfits an opportunity to oppose me. They made it appear to Money that I was the one spreading the rumors on him, which was preposterous on his behalf to think I was. Common sense would tell any sane person that if we have ties under the Bishop set, I was his strength and vice versa. That's like George Bush running around telling the other countries America's army is weak or defected. He'll be sabotaging his own strength. He would never do any shit like that.

Being that Money wasn't a real Blood, and couldn't grasp the realness of being in a gang, he fell into the ploy of the misfits to oppose me. His stupid ass cellie, K.D. from Cabbage Patch Piru supported him.

That evening while we walked to the dining hall, Money was walking in front of me and K.D. was walking in the back. As we got half way inside the rotunda, Money turned around and punches me in the mouth. K.D. simultaneously hit me in my ear. I thank God once again for the remarkable instincts he blessed me with because I immediately started socking Money. By now I'm up against the wall fighting both of them. These two niggas were hitting me so hard and fast, they were like two little bitch ass hyenas on me. It wasn't any love in that rotunda. My busta ass cellie, Daint Dog from Neighborhood 20's didn't come to chow that night. All I could do up against the wall was bob and weave my head side to side to avoid some of the punches so that I could gather my thoughts. They missed a few punches from the result of my bobbing and weaving. That allowed me to quickly exit the rotunda door that was still open to the dayroom. I ran into the dayroom. Money said to K.D. in a hasty voice, "Come on K.D., and let's get him."

They ran into the dayroom after me. Now that I'd gotten a little maneuvering space, it was my time to shine. I went after Money.

It appeared they both became frustrated. Me and Money were throwing punches blow for blow. I knocked him on his ass, he then flew backwards. While on the ground, he was quickly back pedaling his feet from the ground, as though he knew I was going to stomp his ass out. Meanwhile K.D. was about twenty feet away just looking at us. So I decided to go after him, and we both started socking one another in the facial area. By now my arms were tired as hell from all this fighting. K.D. almost dropped me, mostly because I was exhausted.

Finally, the gun tower guard noticed the incident and started yelling for us to get down, and he shot his block gun at us twice. Those niggas got out of that dayroom just as quick as they came in there after me. The COs ran into the section and subdued the situation. They escorted us to the prison infirmary. I sustained a cut inside my lower lip, and a small cut to my right earlobe. The administration put me in the orientation building. Money and K.D. went to the hole (Ad Seg), pending investigation of the incident. I remained in orientation for eight days until they concluded the investigation.

The B-Yard Captain had a couple of his COs handcuff me and escort me to his office. I seated myself in a chair. The Captain asked me what was going on. I replied it was just a fist fight, nothing serious as far as I am concerned. It's over and he can put us all back on the yard together. The Captain stated that he had talked to several Bloods and they didn't want me back on the yard. This Captain was stupid, he actually thought I was some kind of Protective Custody or something. It was obvious he hadn't reviewed my prison file.

"What did you do? Why did they want you?" he asked me.

"Obviously, they don't want me. They are the ones who ran to you about the problem. I didn't ask to see you. You need to send their asses to Protective Custody," I said. And the interview ended, on the words.

The Captain told his Correctional Officers to take me back. I knew all along it was the misfit Bloods who ran to the police. They were scared because they had manipulated the situation. The homie, Rock Bottom from Lueders Park Piru was at his cage door watching the entire event, and he told all of the Bloods on the yard that overall I won. But me and K.D. had a good fight. They put me in Ad-Seg. in three days I appeared before Institution Classification Committee again for the same old bullshit. The committee indicated that I had enemies in both of their facilities and the only option was for them to put me up for transfer to another prison, yet I had documented enemies at each prison. But this was only my initial ICC hearing and I'd see them again on my monthly review for further information. Meanwhile they were going to clear me for the Ad-Seg. Bloods and N-Mexican yard. I had been in Ad-Seg. for three months now pending transfer. Then one day the COs started bringing some Bloods to the section from the C-Yard for fighting each other. As they walked in the section I heard a loud echoing voice calling my name. "Ridah Mike." It was Rat-heem, Ness from Van Ness Gangsta, Weusi from 5 Nine Brim and Big Tee from Inglewood Family Gangsta. Their scuffle were because Ness was pointing out Rat-heem's informant conduct to all of the Bloods on the yard. They put the homie Big Tee in the cage with me. I like Big ass Tee. He came in the cage looking like the actor, Michael Clarke Duncan. Although I liked the homie Tee, but man can he snores. I mean the entire tier could hear him, literally. Tee hit Ness so hard knocking him on all fours. We stayed cellies for two days thank God, and he had the nerve to ask me was it bothering me. Like a damn fool I said no, just trying to be polite.

Rat-heem called me over to the tier and he stated that he need to cellie up with me before he went back to the mainline. So that night Rat-heem came up to my cage and Big Tee went down to cage up with Rat-heem's cellie. Me and Rat-heem stayed cellies for three days. Institution Classification Committee released him and Big Tee back to C-Yard and Ness and Weusi stayed in Ad-Seg. with me.

I told Rat-heem about all of the snitch rumors I heard about him. He vigorously denied it. As he prepared to leave we embraced one another. And he said to me, "Blood, you got a lot of influence with homies use it in a good way." Then he left the cage. In retrospect the only reason he wanted to cage up with me was so that when he went back to the yard he could tell the other Bloods that he was my cellie and that would have confirmed that he wasn't the confidential enemy that prevented me from coming to C-Yard, and to be truthful I didn't think he was. I half-ass started to like Rat-heem in the three days we were cellies. He made me all kinds of promises that when he got back to the yard he was going to do everything within his power to influence the C-Facility Captain. Walker, to let me come to the yard.

That fool had me thinking I was going to go to that C-Yard. I told the Bloods on the Ad-Seg. yard what Rat-heem had told me. And they said if Rat-heem wanted me on C-Yard I would have been out there.

Ness came to our cage during the morning showers. He stood in front of the door taunting Rat-heem. He was extremely hostile. "When you were on the mainline, you were talking shit about Ridah Mike. Now you are in the cell with him all scared and kissing his ass," Ness said.

"No I wasn't, Ness, and that's why we are having problems now because you can't stay out of people's business," Rat-heem responded.

When Ness left our cage Ratheem tried to explain to me that the comments Ness made was his way to set us at odds with each other. I explained to Rat-heem that it wasn't easy to manipulate me to go against anyone. Ness did everything he could to deter me from supporting Rat-heem, but I wasn't biting into the rumors. But he kept trying to convince me that Rat-heem was an informant even after he had went to the mainline.

When Rat-heem left I cellied up with my young Ridah, J-Dubb from Pasadena Denver Lane. I hadn't seen Ness in thirteen years since we were in Old Folsom Security Housing Unit in 1985 and when we departed, we were adversaries. So all the while Ness was trying to influence me to oppose Rat-heem.

I was seriously thinking. Should I put me foot in his ass? Should we make physical contact? Because at this point we were not on the same yard.

One day a brother named Shorty from Oakland sent me an Oakland Tribune newspaper by the request of Ness. The article was pointing out the ongoing violence in New Folsom C-Yard. The prison staff doing the interview clearly denoted Rat-heem's last name, giving him praise by saying he was doing everything in his power to help the Folsom C-Yard staff to maintain a nonviolent facility. I examined the article closely. Everything many Bloods, Crips, and brothers in general were saying about Rat-heem, this article had confirmed it. The COs praised his loyalty to them. The comments the Correctional Officer (CO) made would be beneficial for a life prisoner board hearing. But on the contrary side of the life-style he was trying to portray, he had reduced himself to the rat that he is. In retrospect, the article also strengthened the statements he made to me the first day we met in C=Facility orientation. So I was content with the knowledge of him being an informant.

Ness called me over the tier and said, "That's him (Rat-heem), I told you he was working with the police." Ness finally came over to my yard and we reconciled past differences. Ness is a good homie.

About four months after my incident with Money and K.D., the Bloods on that yard scratched money with a punk ass plastic knife, and knocked him out cold, breaking his jaw and claiming he was an informant. It seemed like everybody who was deceived or manipulated to unjustly go up against me; the wrath of their fate was subject to their nemesis.

Chapter 6

Setting Things Straight

In 1998, I attended the Institution Classification Committee (ICC) orientation for my monthly review. The committee informed me that I was being placed on the transfer list for the California Correctional Institution which was located in Tehachapi, California. I was scheduled to go to the general population on 4B-Facility. I was not allowed in 4A-Facility because, I had a documented enemy.

It's rare that a convict is allowed in the same institution where he has documented enemies.

I guess this was a special circumstance, being that I had documented enemies in every Level 4 180-designed maximum security prison. Therefore they had to compromise with my situation. A month later, a Correctional Officer (CO) informed me that I was indeed on the list for Tehachapi. The following morning after giving the CO my property I lay on my bunk and went into some serious thought.

It had now been nineteen years since I first arrived in the state prison system. I wondered where all the years went. I was nineteen then. Now I was thirty-eight years old. I had no offspring, unless you want to consider the number of young homies I had taken under my wings.

Most of my life, I've only had a few original homeboys who I had the utmost respect for. One has been in prison for twenty-seven years. His name is Elroy. I felt for him and his family. His little brother and nephew, Big and Lil' Squirrel, were killed since Elroy's incarceration. Both of them were my true homies. Big Squirrel was killed by a rival Crip set in the mid 80's. Lil' Squirrel was killed by our homie named Rosko. Word was it had something to do with Rosko being jealous of the ghetto success of Lil' Squirrel. Rosko was later killed three months after killing Lil' Squirrel.

The Bloods, from my knowledge have never been into killing each other. But now, we are starting to act just like Crips. we got a few Blood sets warring against each other. Every single Crip set in Los Angeles has another Crip set for an enemy. It has gotten so bad that the Hoover Crips took the boldest gang stance in L.A. history and decided to renounce being Crips and changed their name to Hoover Criminals and labeled themselves to be Blood and Crip Killers. Anyway, it was very late before I was able to go to sleep. When I awoke, I was mad because the prison bus had left without me. My property was on the bus. One could imagine how I was feeling. I wondered why I was not on the Tehachapi bus. A week had passed before I found out what happened. Institution Classification Committee informed me that I was removed from the Tehachapi list. They said I had an enemy at High Desert State Prison who was no longer there. So instead of sending me to Tehachapi, I would be going to High Desert where I have no enemies. When the COs finally came to my cage to have me pack my property, I became annoyed. I still hadn't gotten my property back from the Tehachapi situation, but the property that I had accumulated from the canteen, I left with my young cellie, Sick Mike from Black P.

Stone and the homie Ardell from 456 Piru.

An hour later, I found myself being escorted to the bus bound for High Desert State Prison. It was a cold day in December. Christmas was just three days away. To put it quite plainly, I had long since stopped caring about holidays. A day was just a day to me. Not that I was uncaring, but reality had set in many years ago. The penitentiary was my reality.

The bus ride to High Desert was seven hours long. It was evening when we arrived. Like every other prison I'd been in, I was forced to endure new arrival procedures. The prison Lieutenant in R & R told us all, "Welcome to High Drama 2. When we finished (R&R) Receiving and Release procedures, I was placed in a cell alone. Two weeks later I was on orientation waiting for bed space in the general population. One night around 10 P.M., a CO came to my cage and informed me that I would be getting a cellie. He said that this new guy was a Blood coming off the bus from Salinas Valley State Prison.

About an hour later, I was looking out of the cage door when I saw this huge ass dude walking up with handcuffs on. He was looking rugged, brown skin, 6'3", and easily weighted 240 pounds. One look wasn't enough, I had to take two. There was a big ass birth mark on the side of his face right by his nose area. It looked as if it covered the majority of his features. Then it occurred to me that this dude looked familiar. That's when it hit me. I realized that I knew this dude, in 1983, while I was at San Quentin.

After removing the handcuffs from him, the escorting COs placed dude in the cage. Dude sat on the toilet that was stationed a foot or two from the door he had just entered. He had a look of surprise on his face. After a moment of silence, he said, "It's been a long time, Ridah Mike." It confirmed that we knew one another. I now remembered that awhile back, I had a stabbing conspiracy against this cat at San Quentin in 1983.

I thought that we were going to have to tear that fuckin' cage up. But when I saw that he had a look of case on his face, I decided not to attack him. we sat there and talked for awhile. Then he settled in and made up his bunk.

During the process, I drifted back to 1983. We were in San Quentin. A comrade named Reno, from 84 Swan, showed some comrades his court transcripts. It indicated that Dog from 80 Swan, Reno crime partner had informed on him. I wasn't on the yard during this occurrence. But when I did arrive there, some comrades approached me and said that there was a rat on the yard. Everybody knew that I despised rats! So after being told that, I asked, "What the fuck is he still here for?"

I was told that Reno wanted to use him in court to clear his name. But one day, I got impatient and had the issue dealt with. Now several years later, certain Bloods seemed to want to put the issue behind us. I personally don't feel that Dog is a rat. I believe now that he just got sloppy drunk, and the police department took advantage of his youth and inexperience. He was coerced into giving the police information. It is a well known fact that the police will use pressure and duress to obtain whatever information they want.

At any rate, my opinion as to why Dog dropped the drawers and gave the police information about Reno, is simply my opinion. Yet most brothers feel once a rat, always a rat. So I have to live by those codes by which we live. It's just difficult to justify how a grown ass man can become a rat. Dude has been functioning within the California Department of Corrections (CDC) system for many years. If I wouldn't have taken the initiative to have him dealt with, then maybe his foul act would have gone unchecked. This is one of the reasons why foul niggas don't want me coming around.

I know that I can't continue to clean up every mess or piece of shit in the Blood world, all on my own. I do acknowledge that with the help of a few chosen breed of solid homies, the task of bringing back the true meaning of Bloodism will be achieved. For those who are truly righteous in the Blood-hood, they know where I'm coming from. There are a lot of homies and people in general who were sold out and ratted on by their so-called homeboys. Yet, they are allowed to roam these prisons without any repercussions. So one can understand my repugnance with those who condone the practice of snitching. Even the California Department of Corrections as well as other law enforcement agencies shares these codes. It's just that they can snitch, and apprehend everyone else, but it's taboo to inform on each other. Occasionally there are good law abiding officials who function in a professional manner.

Sure the slave trade had a major role in breaking the black man's back. The effects of slavery are cycles that continues today. The racist society that has forced itself into our minds, has turned some of us weak, and has turned some of us against our own race. But, we can't continue to pass the blame on a racist society. The genocide of our true selves is something we have to take responsibility for just as well. It should be utterly repulsive for us to sit by and watch ourselves kill each other; turn each other into druggies and rats. We shouldn't be able to do this and not feel the need to react.

Dog and I remained cellies for four months. We both were placed on the main population together. One day Dog asked me who had him stabbed when we were in San Quentin, and I told him the truth. I said me and the rank and file. In which he knew he was probably testing my courage to see if I would own up to my part in the conspiracy of having him stabbed. To be honest I started to really like the dude. We argued and agreed together while we were cellies. I recall in a heated argument Dog saying, "We don't have to do this." He meant argue. I was laying down on my bottom bunk, and I immediately reacted to what I thought was a challenge and began to get up off my bunk. Dog said, "No, not that. We just don't have to talk to each other." That's some real shit! The way I described what happened is true.

I'll never falter when I'm challenged, regardless of the consequences. Big Bow Low was the only cellie I wasn't too hasty to fight who was 6'3 ½" and 240 pounds. He can really fight. Had he dedicated his life 132 to the professional sport of boxing, I believe he would have whipped Tyson & Lennox Lewis' asses. Me and Bow Low once we got into an argument. I said, "Yeah, if we get into a fight in this cage, the TV's going to break and everything else. We are going to have a glass fight in this cage.

If there's any Blood in the California State Prison System more infamous than I am it would be Bow Low. People view him just like they do me, that's why we bonded immediately when we finally met in person in 1994.

Back to me and the situation when we arrived to general population, the prison was on lock down. Dog had just left High Desert and he returned back to this same yard, so he knew everyone on the yard. He told me we had a young twenty-one year old homie on the yard named K.D. from Blood Stone Villain who was the hardest and strongest young Blood on the yard. Now having this in mind, when we were able to program on the yard I bonded with Lil' K.D. and slid him under my wings. I sincerely loved the young homie.

One evening while coming in from the yard K.D. informed me about his cellie named Artie Bo from a Sacramento Blood neighborhood, Del Paso Heights. He pulled an underhanded snake move on him by trying to have him moved from the cell, when K.D. and Artie Bo first caged up together it was agreed for only three weeks. Then K.D. was going to cell up with me because my cellie was going home.

But Artie Bo secretly planned to move to another unit, giving the COs an opportunity to move K.D. to another cell with someone else. So I asked my young trooper what he wanted to do about it. He asked me what I wanted to do. I replied, "It's not on me. It's your decision. I'm just supporting you." It was decided upon that we would both beat Artie Bo's ass. This would mean that once the administration saw this, they would realize that. Artie Bo was not wanted on the yard any longer. This was a ploy commonly tried by most convicts who elect not to work the prison staff to maintain order on the prison yards. Some so-called leaders set up fights, and stabbings per yard lieutenant's and captain's knowledge without having serious penalties imposed against them. But me and K.D. wasn't functioning in such a manner, but we also expected not to go to the hole.

Around 5 P.M. we were walking to the chow hall, and I asked Lil' K.D. had he had enough time to think about the issue and did he still want to carry it out. The young trooper told me in a lecturing manner, "Ridah Mike, we already made our decision; we are going to get him tonight in the dayroom.

When we make a decision we have to follow through with it." I felt extremely proud of him and I immediately realized what Dog had told me about him being the hardest young Blood on the yard.

During the 7 P.M. nightly dayroom activities, our prey got on the telephone to call his family, or someone. While on the phone, a CO told him that he was moving and to go and pack his property. Like cheetahs circling their prey, I head gestured to K.D. to go ahead. He head gestured back indicating the gunner was near the window. I gestured again saying "so." K.D. started it off by walking over to the phone. I got off the bench I was sitting on and headed over to Artie Bo so K.D. and I would get to him at the same time. K.D. hit him in the jaw, knocking him about three-feet backward. Then I punched and grabbed him, knocking him to the ground. Artie Bo curled up in a fetal position while we gave him the ass beating of his life.

The gunner in the tower yelled at us to cease the fighting, but we continued. He fired his block gun. It hit K.D. in the chest and knocked him back a few feet. We separated and lay on the ground.

Because the victim didn't or couldn't fight back, our penalties for our action were assault charges, which carried a Security Housing Unit (SHU) term. Had he fought back we would have all been charged with a mutual combat. That's not a usable offense.

K.D. and I were placed in Administration Segregation pending the outcome of our rules violation report. We were in Ad-Seg. for three weeks. During this time I met a young homie from San Diego,

Emerald Hill. His name was Spank Booty. I liked him, he was a young trooper. I also met two Crips named Frosty from Harlem 30's and Bumper Jace from Du Rocc. They were solid older Crips around my age who shared the same principles as I do. I consider them true homies in this prison life shit.

One afternoon while programming on the Ad-Seg. concrete yard the COs unexpectedly called me and K.D. from off the yard to attend a special ICC the administration was conducting. It was said that they were kicking people out of Ad-Seg. due to overcrowding to make space for the more serious offenses. So they let me and K.D.

return to General Population (GP) by giving us a suspended Security Housing Unit term.

A homie named Too-Tone from Miller Gangster had Artie Bo sign papers to let the administration know that me and K.D. weren't his enemies. This was the only way we could return to that yard while Artie Bo was there. Artie Bo was scary; he knew we were coming back so he moved to the upper yard, but little did he know the COs sent me and K.D. to the upper yard to the same unit he ran to. It was over as far as we were concerned. He got his discipline and that was the end of it. I wrote him a note asking if he had felt that we were wrong for jumping him. we could resolve any issue, one-on-one.

Whomever he wanted to fight with, me or K.D. He replied that he had no problem. But, he decided to go to the administration and tell them he felt it was best that he move to another facility. He's so stupid, he only lasted a couple of months on that yard before three Sacramento homies beat him down again.

K.D. and I moved back to the lower yard where we beat up Artie Bo. The entire Blood society on that yard felt I was wrong, and suggested that I was misguiding K.D. But Dog and Too-Tone were the only Bloods who voiced their opinion to me. I didn't really give a damn about Dog's opinion because of his foul history and Too-Tone only stated that we should not have jumped him.

About two months later, I got into a verbal confrontation with Too-Tone. Then the following day. I told him that because of his insolence, I thought that I was going to have to cut him in his face. He took that as a threat, and socked me on the side of my head real hard. That led into one of the most aggressive fights I ever had. We went blow for blow for at least three minutes. While the Correctional Officers sprayed us many times in our faces with pepper spray.

We both were determined, but I split the middle of his forehead. He hit me so hard in my forehead it knocked me back about four feet, but I quickly got back in there. It was said, that was the best fight ever on that yard. Everyone declared it was a draw. What made Too-Tone so extraordinary was I out-weighted him and had a height advantage. He was 5'7" in height and 170 pounds. I am 5'9" in height and weigh 200 pounds. Because of this incident, I gained a lot of respect for Too-Tone. He didn't panic and run to the police to get me removed from the yard, like so many others have done. We signed some agreement hromos that stated that we could program on the yard together, without any further incidents between ourselves.

A couple of days later, I became involved in another incident. Someone told this informant that I was revealing his past history. While the COs were conducting yard release in front of my unit there was me, Gansta Dee from Neighborhood 20's, BoBo from 59 Brim, Goldie from 30's Piru and Bam from Stockton West Side Blood. K-Nine casually walked over to us and as he approached us, he embraced everyone with a hand shake. I was the last. He reached out to shake my hand and socked me up side my head. He had gloves in his other hand and quickly showed me he had an iron knife in the gloves to scare me because he knew I had chumkems (good fighting abilities). Indeed he was correct. Seeing the knife I started to back pedal as he began to pick up speed, and might I add my back pedaling increased. At this point we were in the grass around the tables. I backed up against a table I didn't see. That allowed K-Nine to make contact. He started swinging the knife hitting me several times in the side rib. I was hitting him as best as I could, which wasn't much, due to my hands being slightly swollen, and finger aching from my fight with Too-Tone. I tripped over a cement slab on the ground that the tables were mounted to, and landed on my back.

This fool got on top of me and started to stab me in the face. All I could do was swing up at his face, and grab his head pulling him close to me to prevent being stabbed in the face with good shots. It seemed as though this was going on for hours, finally the COs came and maced that fool off of me. I had never been so happy to see the police in my whole life.

All of you hard core rappers out there promoting that fearless bullshit to the youth be real with them. I was scared as fuck, and by no means do I consider myself the hardest Blood or brother in the California State Prison System, but as far as documented prison violence is concerned I am amongst the top fifty.

This incident with K-Nine landed me back in Administration Segregation (Ad-Seg). Thank God I wasn't hurt, not one iota. My injuries consisted of scratches, literally. It took about two months to restore my inner strength, because of that incident. I learned to never compromise principles with snitches, they are dangerous because they know they have hidden secrets that could be damaging to them if it's brought to light, and they would react to any threat even if it's bogus.

The Ad-Seg. committee decided to send me to C-Facility. I was placed in a cage with one of my comrades named Big Wacky-Ru. He was from Fruit Town Piru. I was back in stride again. Wack and I remained cellies for about six months. I gained a lot of love for him, he's a righteous brother. But in my opinion, he should be more vicious when situations of indignation occur. I feel, fuck the odds or consequences when it's based upon righteousness. With a body structure of 6'3" and 265 pounds and the fighting abilities he has, he could really shake up some shit. On this new yard, the Blood environment was more unified. There were about 30 of us. In fact, the entire black population on the yard appeared to be in harmony. One afternoon I was amongst some homies exercising at the pull up bars. Me, Lil' Liko from Lincoln Park Bloods, Drack and Tumble, Pacoima Piru Bloods noticed a fight between three or four convicts. I quickly noticed that it was actually a race related fight. I said, "It's racial."

The homies Drack yelled, "Let's go!"

The four of us ran across the yard. We wanted to engage in the fight, so we ran across the yard, this was equivalent to the length of a football field. By this time, the Crips who were on the basketball court saw where we were running to. Tiny Bam from Nutty Blocc C.P.T. Crip who I noticed running to the fight amongst the other Crips. I noticed the homie, Bossman, from Oak Park Bloods running toward the action.

The gunners were yelling get down while at the same time shooting several rounds of projectiles, even the Mini 14. We ignored the bullets being fired.

When we made it to the fight we stated punching everything that wasn't black. I saw an Asian guy and I busted him in the face about five times and dropped to the ground like everyone else to prevent from getting shot. They shot 56 rounds to bring that racial disturbance under control.

While on the ground we laughed when we saw how many brothers failed to get involved. Lil' Compton Crip named Cosmo was lying next to me and said we should get them all. I laughed and sincerely agreed with him, but I didn't push the issue because there were perhaps thirty brothers who we would've had to get. I figured we already had enough black-on-black violence amongst us, to be adding to the problem would be senseless. The High Desert staff took control of the incident and started video-taping everyone who was involved. They wrote our names down and conducted an unclothed body search to identify any signs of injuries and weapons.

Later on we were escorted back to our cages, all except for those who were considered to have caused the incident. Shortly afterwards, I discovered that the incident started when an Asian Disrespected a Crip named Fat Dog from 357, a Crip set out of Pomona. Fat Dog was a tier tender in my unit, he went to the Asian's cage to get something for someone. He asked them did they have whatever it was. The Asian said no. as Fat Dog turned around and walked away, someone in the Asian's cage (cell) said, "I got some dick for him."

Fat Dog turned back and said, "What did you say?" No one in the Asian's cage owned up to the sarcastic remark. So Fat Dog left.

The next day on the yard while Fat Dog and the homie Capone from Nutt Hood Watts Crip were walking laps around the yard, one of the Asian approached Fat Dog and apologized to him, and he got socked in his face. That's what triggered the incident. Fat Dog, Capone, and the Asians went to the hole (Ad-Seg). The next day they came and got my cellie, Liko and sent him back to the hole. After reviewing the video tape and names, they realized that Liko had given them his wrong name. After staying in Ad-Seg. for a month they sent him back to the general population. I needed a cellie so I went to the lower yard to cage up with my Lil' Mexican homeboy J-Mack from Nine Deuce Bishop.

It was now 2000 and I had been in High Desert for two years. It was there when I also met another infamous Blood. His name was Professor Klump. Professor Klump was a huge, fat, greasy looking mutha fucka. He weighed about 310 pounds and stood about 6'4". And I heard from several Bloods that this fat boy can fight. But in my mind I later started to question his fighting ability because I heard that Klump and another homie had some hostile disagreements and the homie called Klump a slob and that was grounds for immediate action on the spot. Calling a Blood a slob or a Crip a crab is equivalent to a white person calling a black a nigger. Klump's infamous reputation was for being scandalous and treacherous. More than fifty Bloods had tried to tell me about Klump's snakish games.

But being that I am the most infamous I know how a lot of dudes will always speak false shit about someone they don't like or care too much about without even knowing that person. Therefore I wasn't too hasty to judge the big fat piece of shit before I had an opportunity to observe him for myself. I had to draw my own conclusion.

Over a period of nine months Klump and I became pretty cool. I have to admit that he was cunning and manipulative. I eventually dropped my guard and became prey to his underhanded and deceitful ploys. One day Klump told me in his slow retarded voice, "Ridah Mike, a lot of homies are scared when you come around because they know they can't do anything foul, but you done your part.

You need to just lay low and let the youngsters step up and do their part." Basically he was trying to give me a pre-warning about what would come later if a continued to be aggressive in our Blood society.

One day Klump sent me a kite (note) explaining that someone had informed him that the jail house snitch named Rat-heem was here at High Desert on the yard.

Klump was enthusiastic about setting a hell of an example on Rat-heem so that all of the jail house snitches throughout the California Department of Corrections would know that High Desert State Prison was not going to tolerate rats. Man, Klump really inspired me, and rejuvenated my spirits. This was the manner I functioned in all of my prison life.

I thought to myself, *"Shit, the Blood society isn't doomed after all. We still got a few Bloods who are functioning in accordance to principles by which we live."*

Klump explained that no one was exempt from our rules. I felt proud of Klump, as would a father teaching his fat little kid to catch a baseball for the first time.

We both agreed that when the right opportunity arrived we were going to smash Rat-heem, before Rat-heem got to High Desert from Folsom. I had previously gotten a letter from Folsom from some devoted comrades enlightening me that they had finally dealt with Rat-heem. Finally, after being on New Folsom C-Yard and working with Captain Walker and the prison staff for thirteen years. When Folsom staff could no longer utilize Rat-heem they transferred his defected ass to High Desert, the lion's den where Ridah Mike was. The first day Rat-heem came out to the yard he brought out a 1030 form. These are papers when someone snitches on you in confidentiality. He let me review the form that indicated someone amongst the Blood society at Folsom B-Yard had ratted on him. While reading the paper and listening to him trying to defend himself, I'm basically thinking to myself, *Shit nigga, after all of the Bloods you ratted on, the last thing that should come out of your foul ass mouth is somebody snitched on you.* During this same period I'd received a letter from Salinas Valley State Prison concerning the Bloods and Crips who had engaged in a melee against each other in that prison. And that a blood named Rat-time had informed on the entire event. I couldn't believe the accusation because Rat-time was one of the solid Bloods in my San Quentin era. He had been incarcerated at that point for nineteen years. I couldn't see him go out like a jail house snitch. So I wrote back to Salinas Valley and I asked my comrades to send me his statements. By now every Bloods and Crips at Salinas Valley were calling him a rat.

A few weeks later the rules violation report arrived to me. I observed it closely and it was incredulously shocking to me, that Rat-time could be that stupid. Me and Big Wacky Ru were cellies once again. During this time both of us didn't believe that Rat-time made the statements that we read, by me knowing the snake underhanded games people play in prison. Prison documents can be false manufactured, because convicts have opportunity to type up those reports. It's their responsibility as their jobs, as prison clerks. So to react on a prison documents could cause someone to be seriously hurt or killed under falsehood, so I asked for his side of the story. And was stunned that Rat-time owned up to making the statements, but he had an explanation for making the statements. He said two other Bloods were supposed to take the case for him, but one of them reneged. I told him I don't consider him a rat, but he's stupid for putting himself in such a vulnerable situation.

It's common that if a person is going to take the responsibility of a case for another, the one who's owning up to the rules of infraction is the only person whose supposed to make statements. It would have been wise that Rat-time tell his Investigating Employee (IE) he had nothing to say about the incident, but this imbecile panicked thinking the prison authority was going to send him to the Security Housing Unit so he started talking like he was Sammy the Bull, the mafia infamous informer.

I figured that we already have a known rat, (Rat-heem) on the yard. Now we had Rat-time's predicament to deal with. Klump who is from 84 Swan and Rat-time from 89 Family Swan, were cellies.

I asked Klump who he felt was best qualified to stab Rat-heem. The comrade that Kiump suggested, I disagreed. I told Klump, "Let's get Rat-time to do it and that would be his redemption from his foul misconduct from Salinas Valley." For one, I seriously thought Rat-time panicked and got scared under a small amount of pressure, a funky year and a half SHU term. So Klump agreed with me. And he told Rat-time about the decision we had reached. Rat-time agreed to do the move, but he said he would like for us to grant him a couple of months before he carried out the assault, so he could make some money before he went to the SHU. We allowed him that privilege. I gave this nigga about five months, and like Dog's snitch situation with Reno back in 1983 San Quentin. I ran out of patience, and gave Rat-time an ultimatum to handle his business or both him and Rat-heem were going to feel the wrath of the menace.

All of the Bloods on the yard, who were involved, knew that I was dead serious, especially Professor Klump. So Klump and Dumb-Mu, a crack head Blood from 89 Family Swan, teamed up with the informants to oppose me. They told Rat-heem that I was plotting to have him hit. They pushed him in a corner where there was no other recourse for him. especially due to the fact that he knew I didn't play games when it came to dealing with such serious crimes of being jail house snitches.

Rat-heem and I got into a battle on the yard. Klump and crack head Dumb-Mu set it up. Rat-time was not present on the yard that cold morning around 8:30 A.M. These suckas didn't realize that Ridah Mike didn't give a flying fuck about going all the way out in a battle. If a nigga wasn't willing to put his life on the line, he needed not to fuck with me. I vowed to myself after the incident with K-Nine that shit would never happen to me again in that manner.

Klump and Dumb-Mu's plan had back fired on their asses because I went berserk on Rat-heem's ass. This fool, who was 6'4" and 270 pounds, was up against me. My heart was and still is much bigger than that nigga's. I had his big ass trying to get the hell away from me while on that yard. He wasn't willing to go all out; big ass pussy.

After the incident, the COs escorted me and Rat-heem to the program office per procedure.

We both agreed that we could remain in the same facility together without having any future problems.

We signed the chromos, stating that we are not enemies. The COs escorted me back to my same cage.

I could have imagined Klump's fat ass must have had a heart attack when he heard that I was back on the yard.

The prison staff sent Rat-heem to the upper yard though we remained on the same facility. That same day, the yard went on lock down for reasons unrelated to the incident that transpired between me and Rat-heem.

A few days passed while we were locked down. A tier tender came to my cage door and slid a note under my door. It was a note from Professor Klump and Rat-time. The note was written in Klump's handwriting and language, but it was sighed Rat-time. The note indicated that the reason me and Rat-heem got into our battle was due to my relationship with Yaribu. I played their games as though I was congruent with their opinion. Then I got myself a big ass piece of iron from one of my partners and made me a knife. And I waited for the police to unlock the yard program. I was going to do a suicide mission on one of them cowards. But we stayed on lock down for a month.

The day the prison officials resumed the yard program, COs came to my cage, handcuffed me, and escorted me to the program office. I didn't know what to think. But when I got there they put me in a holding cage (cell). I saw the homie, D-Roll, from San Diego

Sky Line Piru. He was the Lieutenant's clerk. I asked him if he knew why they brought me down here. he said no, but for me to hold up a minute. He went into the Lieutenant's office. When he came out, he told me the Lieutenant told him, that if I came back to the yard I was going to get into some more shit (fights). So they felt it was best that I be moved to the upper yard and Rat-heem come back to the lower yard with the other rats' with who he is compatible. I looked at the homie D-Roll. I was amazed that these dudes would run to the police for shelter. I said, "D-Roll, these niggas are that scary to go to this extreme to keep me off the yard.

"Look at the other side, it could have been someone who liked you and didn't want to see you get into anymore problems," D-Roll said. That was his theory.

I said in response, "Shit, if a nigga like me, don't rat on me. Help niggas."

I wasn't angry at Klump because I allowed myself to be deceived into trusting a person who I was pre-warned about many times. I knew he was a snake before I met him. It's a snake's nature to bite, so I got bitten. But never in a million years did I think that Klump would oppose me by supporting snitches. He didn't care about Rat-heem, but when it came down to his geographical homeboy Rat-time, that's when he became scandalous. I thought a rat was a rat no matter what geography he is from. When the COs informed me that they were moving me to the upper yard; I asked them if it would be all right if my cellie could come with me. They said if he wanted to, it's all right with them.

My cellie's name was Kirk from Sacramento Oak Park Bloods. We became cellies during the month lock down. Kirk was a strong Blood that would always have my utmost love and support. Two COs escorted the both of us to the upper yard. I was back on the yard where the homies and I had run across the yard to participate in the me-lee with the Blacks versus Asians. When we got to the yard, the homies on this yard heard all of the shots being fired during me and Rat-heem's fight. Being that the gunners shot nineteen times they thought it was a racial riot underway because in prison it's unusual for those many shots to be fired in a mutual combat. But went they learned what had really happened, there were some solid Bloods who were indignant, and offered me their utmost support.

After two months of being on the new yard, Kirk went home. He was in prison for a parole violation. After Kirk left, I was in the cage by myself for about eight days. Then one night a prison bus came in from Ironwood State Prison. I was given a new cellie. He was a young twenty-four-year-old Blood soldier. His name was Solo Bolo, from Circle City Piru, out of Watts. We both lived in Watts, so we had something in common. He was my Lil' Watts's homie. I immediately noticed that Solo was a young Ridah. We became close.

Everything was functioning in tranquility amongst the Blood society and all the brothers in general. One morning on the yard me and about nine young homies were just hanging out on the yard sharing conversation and joking around. One homie made a comment that he heard that the homie Big Suge Knight, Death Row CEO, said Peabody and China Dog were the only two real Original Gangstas (OGs) left. We found that to be hilarious. He wasn't even close.

I don't know where or who he gets his information from, but he needs to examine his source, Because it's obvious that these Bloods who are amongst his circle don't know shit about what they are saying. What about Papa-T from Pueblo Bishop, A' Jene from Bounty Hunter, Miller Moa from Miller Gangsta, Nelly from Inglewood Family, Gangsta Red from 84 Swan, The God Father

L.B. from West-side Piru? Most definitely Meechie from L.A. Dever Lane, the oldest homie in the prison system.

Fifty years old and still a Ridah. And Smokey from Black P. Stone. For one, Peabody has been a total disgrace to the Blood struggle in all his prison life. This dude is an ignominy and homosexual, literally chasing these prison gay boys around. These are degrading examples he has been displaying for the young homies and young brothers abroad, and China Dog never been a factor in the Blood world in prison. But one thing that I didn't like is how he neglected the homie Rock-B from Lueders Park Piru

(LPP). Rock-B sacrificed his whole life for the LPP and Bloods, he should never want for nothing in the prison society.

There are a lot of Bloods hating on Suge, and saying he bought his way into the Blood society.

Personally, I like him and often tell homies to stop hating. I see him as being a street version of what me and Bow Low been going through in prison for many years dealing with these haters. All of the homies should be proud that he's amongst the Bloods' world and uses his success as a motivating force to help us on our paths to achievements and entrepreneurships. But I will say that Blood needs to put more homies in the business. We got homies who are mega talented in the rap game, but haven't been exposed. They are real to what they rap about, unlike a lot of the perpetrators who get all the air play. And when I say this, Snoop and D.J. Quik come to mind. Yeah Quik, you the first that did banging on wax. But that's all of the gang banging you have done, and as far as my comrade J.R. from Tree Top Piru. Quik, all of us real niggas know the Compton police department coerced you into making untrue statements against J.R. on murder charges. However, it's also understood that you were a kid about fourteen when this ordeal occurred. I suggest that you afford brother some legal aid to rectify his conditions. And Snoop, on wax you are the ultimate Crip. Man, you need to take some off of that shit. Everybody in the world knows you a Crip. The vast majority of these hardcore young bangers view y'all as bustas. But my purpose is not to add to our plight, but to be a positive solution. When rappers promote drive-bys and senseless killings in our communities, real ghetto Ridahs (gangstas) believe that driving by and killing children, elders and innocent people are for cowards. I'm not promoting violence, but a real mutha fucka will hunt his prey down and handle his business like a man. It seems as though you brothers don't have any sympathy for the same community who made you the success you are. You move your families away from the senseless killings, but we are still there struggling day to day.

Chapter 7

Fighting Amongst Ourselves to Fight for Ourselves

On July 10, 2001, during a facility search, this CO at High Desert State Prison discovered the knife that I brought with me from the lower yard. I had it concealed in my A.C. adapter. It had been there for about six months. I had been through a few major searches prior to this one. But something kept telling me to get rid of it. I was puzzled and uncertain about it, so I asked the little homie Solo for his opinion. He said to follow my first thought. However he didn't think that they would find it. Since they couldn't find it in the previous searches, I was content with the answer he offered me and left it inside the adapter.

The H.D. searching staff finally made their way to my section. Two COs came to me and Solo cage. They instructed us to strip our asses naked for a body search, then handcuffed us, and escorted us to the unit dining hall. Where they put all of the convicts during cell searches. Solo and I entered the dining hall. We noticed two other

Bloods sitting at a four man table; their names were Pee-Wee from Lueders Park Piru and Bad News from Pasadena Denver Lane. We sat at the table with them. The COs were in both of our cages for a long time exceeding the normal time it takes to search a cage.

I started to get kind of leery and began asking them questions about do they think the police found my weapon? They were like, "Don't trip." (not to worry).

The COs finally came and got them. They were escorted back to their cage. Solo and I remained at the table by ourselves. I began to really feel uneasy by now. The only thing that kept going through my mind was that I should have gotten rid of that knife. My mind set was that whenever I went back to the SHU I'd rather it be for stabbing somebody who deserved it, not for having a knife violation.

After waiting in the dining hall in handcuffs behind our backs for approximately four hours, the Sergeant and two other Correctional Officers came to Solo and me asking us to stand to our feet, and they escorted us to the pro9gram office. While walking they didn't say anything to us about the knife being discovered, but it was enough evidence to know that they had found it.

The COs who conducted the search didn't find it. The facility property CO Big-ford found it.

He normally checked the appliances for broken seals. Particularly televisions and radios. He showed up unexpectedly checking all kinds of shit.

Once they got us in the program office, they put us in the small holding cages next to each other.

I told Solo don't worry about it. They took us in an office room separately for questioning and read us our rights. We were charged with possession of a prison manufactured weapon that can carry judicial penalties. This meant nothing to me. The only thing that would affect me was to send me back to the SHU for ten months. But on the contrary, Solo had his whole life to lose, for something he had nothing to do with. He could go back to court and if found guilty he would receive his third strike, giving him life in prison. So when I went into the office for questioning I took full responsibility for having the weapon.

I also had done the same when we had our 115 (Rules Violation) hearing. This jack-ass Lieutenant still found Solo guilty as charged. That fucked me and Solo up. I felt terribly bad and Solo was in a nervous wreck. He had always felt that if he got life it would be for something he done himself.

I knew that Solo would eventually be vindicated because there was no evidence against him.

Also my admission cleared him. Normally, convicts beat cases when their cellies accept the charges.

Later, after reviewing the Lt.'s findings, the Facility Captain overruled the Lt.'s finding against Solo. The charges were dismissed. My SHU term for the weapo9n remained the same. This was the best thing that came out of this situation because Tehachapi was only two hours away from my home.

I hadn't seen my mother in fifteen years. She often wanted to come visit me while I was at Pelican Bay and High Desert, but I told her no, it was too far away. Anyhow, Solo went back to the mainline (general population). I waited in Ad-Seg. pending transfer to Tehachapi Security Housing Unit (SHU). When Solo left my comrade Bam-bada and I cellied up. Bam was from Out Law 20's. He was one of the most percolated and authentic Bloods I've encountered in a long time.

His mental and physical valiance was far beyond average. Bam was 6'3 ½" and 255 pounds, solidly built. Bam loved doing exercises, because he was once fat. He was a brownish-dark complexion, with maybe two inch dreadlocks he just started to form. We both exercised and studied together. During our exercise period, while I was doing my set of push-ups and curls, Bam would be reading a book out loud. And once I was done I would read where he stopped while he's doing his set. We done that until the exercise was completed for about a little over an hour.

On this Ad-Seg. yard; there were twelve Crips and seven Bloods, three Black Guerilla Families and the rest of the brothers were nonaffiliated. The entire yard exercised together. There was a sense of common unity amongst all of the brothers on the yard. Ever since I've been on this yard there were Crips leading the exercise machine as instructors. At this point I've been on this Ad-Seg. yard for three months.

And every time an instructor left Ad-Seg. he would be replaced with another Crip. So one day my BGF partner named Heshima, an ex-Blood from San Diego was placed as the second instructor. This enraged the homie T-Ball from Black P. Stone who I've known since he was nineteen years old. He's thirty-six now and I was forty. T-Ball told me he feels that the Crips and Black Guerilla Families were playing underhanded politics with the exercise program. He had been on this yard longer than all of these dudes participating and enthusiastically supported it and they had not offered him the responsibility of instructing. So he told me, "Blood, I'm not exercising with them anymore." "Neither am I, but I didn't tell the other Blood's not to exercise, it was their decision." But they all followed me and T-Ball example except Gangsta Dee from Neighborhood 20's. He was an exercise fanatic anyway.

The exercise formation was called, everyone assumed position except for me, T-Ball and four other Bloods. The six of us was in the front of the yard doing push-ups. The normal proc ؛dure in the group exercise would be to run laps before starting the calisthenics. So while they were running around the yard, T-Ball told Ricc Rocc from 8-Ball Hustler Crip, he got to talk to him about running in back of us. Ricc Rocc response was, T-Ball you know that the exercise machine has priority on the yard, which is true. T-Ball responded in disagreement. By now the entire yard had stopped running and everyone started bickering and voicing their opinion about what's transpiring. Bloods on one side of the yard and Crips on the other. Some opinions was getting hostile, now the yard is tensed, my young Compton Crip Ridah named Bam eased up to me and said Hubb and Dubb which mean Compton and Watts together.

He was indicating that if it go down on the yard, me and him would avoid fighting each other. I smiled at him. Everyone continued to bickerer. Bam hastily walked into the middle of the yard and said in a voice of rage, "If anybody out here not for black unity, step your ass up to the mic! And I will break your ass in two!" Ricc Rocc was leaning against the wall, he replied, "Bam that's on 8-Ball Hustler Crip!

You are not going to break me in two!" Bam said, "This is Outlaw 20's. Step your ass up to the mic then!" Bam took steps towards Ricc Rocc. And Heshima or T.C. got in between Bam to prevent his advancement towards Ricc Rocc all the while the gunner is in the tower trigger happy and eager to let off some rounds. Finally everyone regained their composure. Like true brothers we reconciled our conditions on the yard, and continued to group exercise in harmony. All except Ricc Rocc. I felt bad that I allowed the homie T-Ball to influence me to succumb to personal loyalty against black unity. Afterward he felt that I was angry at him, I was, but I wasn't going to oppose him.

The next day after the intense situation, the COs came to me and Bam's cage and informed me to pack my property because I was on the bus list to be transferred to Corcoran. He denoted that I would be staying at Corcoran Security Housing Unit for maybe two months as an enroute for Tehachapi SHU.

Around 2 A.M. they came and escorted me to R&R. The bus was headed to our destination around 3:30 A.M. There was one other Blood on the bus with me. His name was Dollar Bill from Neighborhood 20's. We were weary most of the 7 hour ride. So we slept in a sitting position for most of seven hours. We were put in a very small cage in front of the bus.

When we arrived at Corcoran, we were taken off the bus. As I stepped off the bus some intoxicated looking Mexican Sergeant was very hostile towards me, he tried to look hardcore. He said welcome to Corcoran as he instructed me to spread my legs as wide as I was able, hands planted on the top of my head. I didn't know what to think or, why out of thirty plus convicts on the bus, I'm the only person being harassed?

After that brief harassment two civilized Mexican Correctional Officers (COs) escorted me into R&R. I asked them what was that all about? They laughed and said they didn't know, and he never did that before. We were body searched and placed in holding cages. Then they gave us our clothing and bed linen. While in R&R I noticed there was a Black Lieutenant, and he also looked like he was drunk as well. The Sergeant who initially harassed me was fascinated at how long I had been in prison. I guess he looked in my file that was on the bus and realizes I still had a little fire left in me, because he said he noticed that had a C-Number that indicates the length of a person's incarceration. He became amiable and said that he was not going to give me a hard time, and he expected me to do the same in regards to his Correction Officers. I said, "Sergeant, I was here in 89 when Corcoran was a real prison, now it's a Protective Custody prison, like all the rest of them." He nodded his head in agreement. I told him that I was only here temporarily, and that I was an enroute for Tehachapi Security Housing Unit (SHU). He told me that it'll take me about six months before I leave.

At about 11 P.M., we were being escorted to the building we were assigned to live in. we were all going to a cage by ourselves, until we went to ICC in the event they allowed us to double cell. As I stepped into the section walking to my cage on the second tier, I heard a loud voice calling my name,

"Ridah Mike." I said in my normal reply, "Yeah, what's happening?" "Who is that?" He yelled back,

"Vertis." I stated in elation, "What's up homie?" We conversed over the tier for about ten or twenty minutes about things that would be generally discussed over the tier. He embraced me with a care package that consisted of toothpaste, soap, lotion, and some Top Ramen Soups.

I've known Vert since 1979, when I first came to the Los Angeles County Jail. The incident I experienced when my nose was split, Vert was one of my supporters. He was an O.G. East Coast Crip four or five years older than I. He became frustrated with the Crip world and relinquished all his gang ties. \The final straw was at High Desert in 1998 when his lil' homies from East Coast Crip teamed up on him and knocked out all of his front teeth. It was said that he disrespected one of them.

I stayed in the cage for a month alone, on walk alone status that mean you can only go to the yard by yourself. About ninety-seven percent of Security Housing Unit was n this status. Everyone who has an assault was subject to this status. They are so stupid you couldn't even go to the yard with your won cellie. I found that to be ridiculous.

After a month of being by myself a CO came to my cage and wanted to know if I would go down to the program office and talk to a Blood who was in another section, to see if we were compatible to cell up with one another. He handcuffed me and escorted me to the program office holding cage. The other Blood was already in a holding cage located directly in front of the one I was in. He had on some big asses' bifocals. We were around the same size all the way around. He said, "What's up Blood? I'm Poppa C.K. from Van Ness Gangsta." I said, "I'm Mike from 9 Duce Bishop. I don't really want any cellie. I'm just a lay over, and I will be going to Tehachapi SHU any day now." We briefly talked about whom we knew.

Finally, I said to Poppa, "Blood they call me Ridah Mike."

He responded by saying, "I've heard of you."

I said, "As far as cellies are concerned I don't want one, but it's on you if you want to cell up with me, we can do that."

He said to me, "If you are who you say you are, I will like to cell up with you so that I can get put up on some things (to be abreast)." I knew right then that Poppa was a young Ridah because if he had not been a soldier, he wouldn't even had considered being amongst my environment with the infamous reputations.

Having Poppa as a cellie was alright. We had a great deal in common. We stayed cellies for two weeks before the police unexpectedly came to our cage at about 2 A.M., and told me that they will be coming back to get me in about thirty minutes for Tehachapi Security Housing Unit (SHU). They came back around the stated time and I embraced Poppa with a huge hug and encouraged him to remain strong.

I was once again headed on my way, like so many other times before. They put me and an older brother in a white barred van. It was a forty-five minute drive. When I made it to the Tehachapi SHU, there wasn't a Blood in that entire building. The next morning the floor Correctional Officer (CO) noticed that I was a new arrival. He asked me what was I affiliated with, I said the Bloods. He said that there was no Blood yard on this SHU. Facility because the Bloods and Northern Mexicans were involved in a melee against each other and the administration sent all of the Bloods to B-Facility SHU.

He also told me that when I attend Institution Classification Committee within the 10 days procedures, they would endorse me to go to forty-eight yard SHU the Blood compatibility yard.

I was on walk alone status once again, as the CO informed me ICC was transferring me to B-Yard. It would be two months sitting in this cage waiting to go to forty-eight yard that looked like it wasn't going to happen. Prior to being moved, I talked to Sergeant Garza about transfer concerns. He checked it for me and told me that ICC had cancelled my transfer to B-Yard, and he was in process of making another Blood yard here in 4-A Security Housing Unit about two weeks after talking to Sergeant Garza he had established a Blood yard in unit 6. I was sent to that unit to cellie up with a young Blood named B-Dawg from Pasadena Denver Lane. Three weeks of being cellies B-Dawg went to the mainline.

During my two months these homies were some of the most dysfunctional imbeciles I've been around in a long time. Not in the sense to where they were weak and cowards, in my opinion, they were all soldiers. They were just too aggressive and disorganized. They had no discipline, in regards to Blood love, unity, and a sense of functioning in a consolidated manner it was remote. I had to beat them with rage, just to get them to exercise and stop arguing to the point where they were about to throw blows, over a basketball game. I once grabbed the basketball and threw it over the wall, and told them if they start fighting the first person who threw a blow, I was going to run over there and bust him in his head.

I met the homie Big Curt Dog, from 62 Brim. I was forty-one at the time and he was forty. I really admired Curt for being a strong Blood at forty, and he still had fire in him. He told me once, a lot of these older dudes take the fire out of these youngsters and water them down so hard. It's impossible to ignite the fire needed to help them become soldiers, or to keep their soldiership.

We were both in congruence once we started to speak about how it's a shame that niggas be hating on each other. Curt said, "Ridah Mike, a person can kill five mutha fuckas, and those haters are still going to hate him, and say he should have killed six." Curt stressed this point to say you can't please niggas who hate. For those who don't understand the infamous lifestyle. If a person was as violent as the example Curt Dog described in the infamous lifestyle that would be equivalent to a legal professional person achieving their highest goal. So that's why he gave me such a hideous example to show that people are going to hate you no matter what you do.

On April 11, 2002, my SHU term had expired from the High Desert knife violation. As a result, I was released to the 4-A mainline (general population). I was placed in 4-A, 4C-Section that was for orientation, pending ICC and clearance for the yard. On my ninth day in orientation, I still wore the SHU white jumpsuit, everyone else was wearing blue prison jeans and shirts.

During the morning breakfast, I entered the dining hall, and I stood out like the Supreme Court Justice Judge Clarence Thomas at a Ku Klux Klan rally. The homie Dee BoBo from 59 Brim noticed me and waved through the kitchen window. The same day, the entire yard knew Ridah Mike was in orientation.

Twenty-three years later, and these dudes are still panicking and running to the administration to keep me from coming to the yard, but it was to no avail. I hadn't violated any rules. It was obvious these dudes were scared, and didn't even know me personally. There were couples of homies who knew me personally, or heard of me, and spoke up in my favor. That outweighed the criticism the haters spoke about me. The first day I went to the yard my lil' dog Baby Laniak was right by the door waiting for me to come out, the last time I had saw him he was eighteen years old at Folsom. Now he was twenty-two.

I embraced the lil' homie and he was as firm as ever, still a young Ridah. He told me he been hearing about me, and that he heard about me getting stabbed at High Desert by K-Nine, and he heard basically I was disfigured from the result of that incident, I started laughing. I said, "Laniak do you have a microscope on you? Because that's the only way you can see my injury." He started laughing and we started walking. I met his cellie Young Gangsta T-Way, another young twenty-two-year-old Ridah who had heard about me. I stayed on the yard with these two young homies only for one month. They both was charged with a stabbing assault on a CO. It was said the CO called me as well as many others to their office. The Lieutenant told me how all of these dudes were sending him notes trying to keep me off the yard when I was on orientation. I said I already know, he told me he knew I wasn't involved in the young homies assault on his Correctional Officer. But he felt that my presence on the yard inspired them to carry out such actions.

Baby Laniak and T-Way were young Ridahs way before meeting me. And might I add they are some intelligent young men as well. They are hardcore young Bloods but race conscious.

In 2002, while at Tehachapi Security Housing Unit (SHU), I finally had the opportunity to see and visit with my mother. She has been my only and utmost unconditional love, and strength. Over a decade and a half had passed since I last saw her in person, before this visit. There was transition from maintaining an impregnable demeanor to one that encouraged me to embrace a loved one. This unprecedented reformation also helps me to see the reality of reunification with my mother. This aspect of life appeared within my sight. I had long since stopped liking my brothers, sisters, cousins, nephews, and nieces, but I loved them only because it was a biological thing to do. People claim that they love you, but love is demonstrated by action and deeds, not just words only. Generally speaking, how can you say you love someone and sit around and watch them suffer without offering them moral support. That mean you your love is hollow and vain.

My mother was accompanied by my youngest sister Dorine, and my second to the youngest sister, Jacqueline. Dorine was at the mere tender age of eleven when I last interacted with her. Now she is thirty-six years old, a mature, beautiful woman who is married.

She has two young boys of her own, two foster sons, who are our biological first cousins. She is an elementary school teacher in one of L.A.'s poverty-stricken, inner city schools, and is pursuing a doctoral degree.

There were only two things that my little sister said she remember about me. One was a song she said I use to always play, "Strawberry Letter 22," by the 70's group "Brothers Johnson". The other thing was that she said she hated the way in which I used to thump her forehead with my fingers. She said I used to do that when I was mad. I remember it vividly. My intention was to be irritating, not out of anger, but I always had a disgruntled sense of humor.

My sister Jacqueline has matured as well. She is a beautiful, mature woman and is now thirty-eight years old. I last saw her when her first child Jennifer was 3 ½ years old. The year was 1986. I was in Old Folsom State Prison (SHU). Jacqueline is now married, has two boys and two girls, and is proudly serving our impoverished community as a pre-school teacher.

The lost years became prevalent and evident in a matter of minutes. My mother was now sixty-seven. It seemed as though she had aged over night, yet she was stable. I didn't anticipate the physical change in her being that I talked on the telephone with her as often as I could. I've always envisioned her as being the same as I last saw her, but the cliché holds true: 'Time stands still for no one.'

The visiting area we met in was like a hallway with seven phone booths lined up side by side, concrete and a thick Plexiglas window which kept the visitors from having physical contact with the prisoners. Each booth had small dime size holes at the bottom of the metal slab. The holes allowed us to communicate with each other.

Two COs escorted me to the visiting booth to greet my family. I calmly, yet anxiously waited twenty minutes or so for the reunification with my existence. My mother walked in. I recognized her immediately. Then my two sisters appeared behind her. Before the visit, I had been in the Security Housing Unit (SHU). Consequently I appeared rough, rugged and a bit beyond recognition.

My mother, in her soft, curious voice said my name as if she were asking me a question. She squinted her eyes, tilted her head and cautiously walked closer to the chair positioned in front of her son.

She burst into tears and began to cry aloud. I tried to maintain my composure but my buried emotion came alive on the inside of me. Then I felt the tears trickle down my face. I sobbed out of love for my mother. Emotions that I hadn't shown my entire life were now evident. I remember telling my mother, "I'm only living for you. I don't care about nothing in this world but you."

My sister Jacqueline tried to console my mother and repeatedly said, "Don't cry." I'm sure she felt my mother's pain. After about ten minutes we all regained our composure and proceeded in general conversation about family things that I was curious about.

The limitation of our one hour visit passed by as if it we only twenty minutes. My hour was ending when a white female CO politely told my mother and sisters that they would have to leave in ten minutes. My mother instructed us to close the visit with prayer. We bowed our heads and my youngest sister led the prayer. Afterwards, we embraced through comforting words and placed our hands on the glass window to mimic physical contact. After savoring the last cultivating vision of my existence, I was escorted back to my cage.

Although I am physically caged, for the first time in a long time I really felt necessary. I became reacquainted with the emotions of life, and it felt good. With the prison life and experiences deeply embedded in my mind, I felt that if anything were to happen to my mother, I would end my life by committing a kamikaze attack on anyone who enraged me at such a moment. However, seeing my mother and two sisters made me realize that maybe I should stay out of these prison holes (SHU) and get to know my family, especially those I have never had the pleasure of meeting.

I've became acquainted with a newfound bond with a nephew who wasn't born when I was last in society. His name is Baby James,

(BJ). B.J. is the sixth child of seven by my oldest sister, who has been having drug problems all of her life, as well as her husband.

I am proud to say B.J. is not involved in drugs or affiliated with gangs. In the neighborhood he lived in, not to be affiliated can be interpreted as having a great sense of personal integrity and courage.

B.J. is a twenty-one-year-old independent young brother who possesses the valor of a Ridah. He's wise enough to use his talents in a legitimate way. I'm sure he'll do well with his beautiful fiancé, Calisha and their young son, who I consider my only real family amongst my mother.

I've shared letters with B.J., Calisha and I endeavor to express my beliefs about the Jewel of life that they have gained. It is important for him to know that a family with a strong man of his stature is genuine. B.J. once expressed to me in a letter that he has never had a positive male figure around. In his own words, Quote "So a nigga had to be his own man" End Quote. I felt extremely proud of him. but at the same time I felt ashamed of myself for not being there for him.

Many of us older brothers have disillusioned our youth, and in some cases to the point of no return. We have neglected the priorities of being a man. First and foremost to our women, children and family unit as a whole. I have gone through my trials and errors, and as many of you can relate, I have taken the responsibility to set a positive example for other young men. A person's doesn't have to come down this road to discover that prison life is a cruel type of life to live. I am certain that B.J. and Calisha would be a positive solution to the senseless plight that exists in our communities. When I think of them, I often ponder about the well being of other young brothers and sisters in our society.

It really disturbed me to see the news anchor reporting the death of the young prominent actor, Merlin Santana, a.k.a. Romeo, of the Steve Harvey television show. It was a senseless killing, committed perhaps by some young idiot who wanted to be a gangster, or whose existence was no greater than selling and smoking crack, or some other drug. The situation sickened me because Santana was striving to become someone great in his life. It's sad that our community has to constantly lose young prominent brothers and sisters (especially those who chose to avoid the infamous path) because of choices someone with a troubled lifestyle made.

My purpose is not to gash up on the young Ridah, because I was once you, but if you continue your reckless path of life, you will soon be me. The harsh reality of life is that you may not be as fortunate as I have been. A lot of brothers in our neighborhoods and in the entertainment field glamorize or embellish the so called gangsta life. But, it's not what they claim it to be. It's a fucked up life to live.

I'm not trying to use euphemistical words to insinuate anything different. It's as harsh as I stated.

This is one of the reasons I prefer the usage of the word cage instead of cell. We are caged like animals, sometimes for months or years without any yard, and they wonder why we're crazy. I prefer not to address police or COs as officers, because the vast majority of them do not deserve that title of honor.

They are more corrupted than we are. There are dramas against fellow prisoners, who you make think are your true homies, there are racial and group dramas amongst your own race, being mistreated by degrading prison administrating procedures; enduring the evil games some prison COs play as they hide behind the so-called badge of justice. So if you desire to live this type of life, believe me, the judicial system will be honored to find a cage for you. Acknowledge this fact: If there is no one to occupy these cages, prison officials and the judicial system would be unemployed. Your troubled lifestyle is their livelihood.

I'm sharp enough to know that after this long journey of imprisonment, a person must be cautious of who he makes sacrifices for. All of my prison incidents were related to making sacrifices for the justice of others. I conduct myself too discreet to be getting into personal conflicts. Many will perpetrate the loyalty role, but in the moment of a crisis they will falter, or dastardly turn against you. A true man and a warrior knows that it is wiser to be among hundred so f loyal, genuine, and valiant and principle functioning individuals, than to be among thousands of pseudo, and mercenary functioning people.

It is only by unity that we can set on a journey to change some aspects of the way we live and treat each other in our race. There are far too many of our children, mothers, fathers and homies dying in a war that lacks meaning and purpose. I hope that all brothers and sisters will soon join together and fight the real war which is the one against oppression and injustice for all people.

As Bloods and Crips, we're a powerful entity in this nation. We are national. We exist in more than forty states, and we will continue to exist no matter who tries to abolish our existence. I would never tell homies not to Blood or Crip, but to strive to build it, to uplift our communities. It is our responsibility to raise ourselves to a higher and more positive level. Bloodism and Cripism are only tribes. African tribes have been existing for centuries.

You must enhance your own mind by making yourself the best individual you can be. When I first came to prison I couldn't read or write. The only thing I could spell was three or four letter words.

Though I have a violent prison history while locked up in these cages, I taught myself how to read, write and spell. So, I consider myself a self-scholar person, and striving to be erudite. Since I took the time to educate myself; it enables me to put my life on paper. If everyone took this approach you would be elevating yourself to being sharp and that would makes you a positive example for your neighborhood and your race.

I was able to venture into the 1800's. I learned about our beloved slave Nat Turner. He was a preacher who defied slavery boldly by leading a slave army, marching from plantation to plantation destroying slave masters and recruiting slaves who had the desire to be free and treated like human beings. Though his war didn't end in triumph, he established the idea in the slave owners' minds that niggas would stand up and fight for their human rights. A lot of brothers glamorize and praise the deceased mafias, Al Capone and John Gotti; they weren't anywhere near as hard as Nat Turner.

If you just have to praise white heroes, praise the 1800's abolitionist John Brown who was a righteous and brave man who also looked slavery in the eye and refuted it boldly. He sacrificed his own life as well as his family for human rights. On his way to his hanging death, he saw a little black girl and kissed her and said God bless you. So tell me, was Nat Turner and John Brown Ridahs? Fuck Al Capone and John Gotti, they didn't give a damn about black folks. They poisoned our communities with drugs that's about all they done for us, and left us this self-destructive gangsta legacy. So it's on us to take this gangsterism shit to a level that's helpful to our communities.

A lot of us say in the gang wars there has been too many deaths to begin to reconcile past strifes.

I say the white supremacist killed more than two million Africans in our slave trade history. Today we are still dying as a result of plantation psychosis (a severe mental disorder resulting from slavery). Those slave owners were forgiven, as well as their offspring who inherit the power that be today, so why can't we forgive each other?

Whether we have the fortitude to comprehend it or not, doesn't change the fact that we are a political party that is in great shambles. We put our lives on the line for red, blue, Blood, and Cuz language and try to control some dilapidated crack house or neighborhood that really doesn't belong to us.

All the while our youth's future is being sabotaged. They follow our blighted path, while the democrats and republicans gang bang against each other in a more sophisticated manner.

Political parties control the country, world, and create laws that regulate our lives. We have to focus on the overall level. Fuck trying to control a broken down drug house. Say we decided to legally politicize Bloods and Crips. Our families would be eager to support us. There are Bloods and Crips in entertainment, professional sports, army, marine, air force and many other legal and prospering professions in the country. If we genuinely started to transform our negativity into righteousness that will uplift our communities, I'm certain they will support us, but as long we are a threat to ourselves and the communities, we shouldn't expect their support. Together we could give a new meaning to the word "Menace to Society," instead we can become a menace towards injustice. I once saw a conference on television of the billionaire Ross Perot reform party. This was the most dysfunctional political gathering or meeting I had ever seen. If the reform party can enter the political field, surely Bloods and Crips can.

I am optimistic about our future. I'm sure there are like-minded brothers in the gang world who share these principles. I don't believe in the adage, if I can save one life, I'll be satisfied. This concept will not help or save us when we are dying at an alarming rate. We need thousands and millions. Let me show a small example of hope:

On July 3, 2003, during the 7:30 P.M. program in the dayroom, my lil' road dog Kick Back (KB) from Campanella Park Piru, was being forced by the COs to pack up his property and move to another block in a cage with another person he didn't know. K.B. tried everything within his legal rights to compromise, he even asked could he talk to this guy before caging up with him to see if they were compatible, but in their tyrannizing manner they wasn't concerned about his well being, or his living conditions. Sergeant Blaylock was the most blatantly racist CO I has seen in a long time. To describe him would be a modern day Hitler. He once threatened to shoot me in the head if I had walked up to the second tier. Anyway, he was the source of this problem.

My young Ridah K.B. decided not to give the COs the satisfaction of placing him into a compromising position, so he refused to move. At this particular time there were three Bloods, ten Crips and one Hoover. We all banded together in support of K.B. We thought they were going to come inside the dayroom and physically remove him, so we decided not to lock up in our cages to prevent such an act.

They had something else in mind. After maybe twenty or thirty minutes of trying to verbally force us into our cages; they started to impose chemical warfare against us. Finally they took control of the situation. I've dealt with the Mini 14's, shotguns, and now chemical agents that would make you wish you were shot instead.

We were all placed in Ad-Seg. pending the outcome of the rules violation report, by which the unprofessional manner Blaylock and other ranking officials conducted this incident. A higher authority reduced our offense to a lower level, not warranting us a SHU term, all except K.B. due to their belief that he was the inciter.

On September 11, 2003, I appeared before ICC. A-Yard Captain Lopez done everything within his power to prevent me from returning to A-Yard. He said in earnest to Mrs. Todd the Assistant Warden, word was amongst the inmates that I could have stopped the incident. So basically he wanted to punish me for not catering to his staff.

There were two options for me. Send me to another yard, B-Yard, or transfer to another prison.

Either one was fine with Captain Lopez, but not to send me back to A-Yard. Being that I had documented enemies in every Level 4 180-designed maximum security prison, in which I was only eligible for, CSR (a higher authority than the prison) was more than likely going to deny a transfer due to the enemy situation. I would have been sitting in Ad-Seg. for months or perhaps a year pending transfer and waiting for enemies to leave a prison so that I would be able to go there, but my counselor, CC II Mrs. White suggested to Mrs. Todd that I go back to A-Yard. Captain Lopez became belligerent, but she stuck to her suggestion and it gave Mrs. Todd a momentary incentive, and finally she rendered her decision. She said, "O.K., I'm sending him back to A-Yard." Captain Lopez loo9ked and said dejectedly my word don't carry any weight with her. She responded by saying yes Captain Lopez, your word carries a lot of weight with me, with a facial expression and grin that indicates I got to do what I feel is best. I appreciate the support Mrs. Todd and Mrs. White afforded me so that I can continue to visit my mother and bond with my family. Like Nat Turner and John Brown, though we couldn't win the battle, we was heard, and perhaps before they decide to exercise their power upon people in a dictating way, maybe they would consider taking another route in dealing with people. Well at least those who are willing to rebel against oppression. There are brothers like Young Ridah from Water Gate Crip and Peanut from C.P., C.P.T. Crip who gives the struggle hope. I am presently back on IVA Tehachapi yard with my new cellie Gangsta Winn, another young homie who I've bonded with. Obviously he's a Ridah. Despite all of the drama we been through in this cage with each other, our bond remains strong.

As I conclude my journey of speech, I would like to say as an O.G. (Old Generation or Original Gangsta) which ever you prefer to term it, I vow to our oppressed communities that I will continue to be a positive catalyst in fighting the blight and injustice that we impose upon our communities and ourselves.

Bloodism and Cripism is Los Angeles based, not that we are harder or better than the other homies throughout the nation, but let us ask the positive example for the millions of homies and brothers abroad.

Let's stop the senseless killings of our people.

My dream and desire is to see all of the O.Gs. Y.Gs. B.G.'s Baby Locs,' Rascals, and Babas' see with the eyes of change and unity. This is not only addressed to Bloods and Crips. This message is also sent out to the Latinos, Whites, and Asian gangs that participate in this infamous lifestyle that only leads us to two places: Prison or Graves.

Appendix

Letters to my Holy Mom

ADDEND

Vitiligo

Dear Mom,

First and foremost as always, I trust and pray that when you receive this missive it finds you and everyone well and in good spirit. I am doing pretty good myself, mind and body under my circumstances.

Mom, I was just sitting back reminiscing about the last times we saw each other in physical form.

And I decided that I would relinquish my cathartic thoughts to you in the form of corresponding. I was thinking about the time you and Dorine visited me in 2002 when I was in Tehachapi prison. At the conclusion of the visit when I embraced Dorine and you,

you curiously asked me, "Michael, what is that white spot below your lip?"

"I don't know, I think it's from lack of sunlight," I replied. I had been in the Security Housing Unit (SHU) and in isolation for so long during my incarceration that it prohibited me from getting the appropriate, natural sunlight needed to mange one's skin complexion. So I assumed that my pigmentation (particularly facial and hand areas) were pale resulting from the lack of sunlight, which I believe was partially right.

I also thought that when I bathed I usually washed excessively hard and assumed that could have been an additional factor to the lightening of my skin condition. I recall in 2007 asking my young cellmate, Smokey did he think I was scrubbing my skin color away. The twenty-one-year-old educated a forty-seven-year-old (me) with common sense, "You can scrub your skin color away," he said. I never paid too much attention to my condition because my main perception of it was a lack of sun.

However, during a third trip back to Pelican Bay State Prison SHU where I reside currently, I was housed in a cell next door to a Southern Mexican named Speedy, who I befriended.

Speedy had Hepatitis-C that he contracted at a young age in society. He was twenty-eight years old when we met.

His medical condition was grave. "There are four stages to this disease before it becomes fatal," Speedy explained during our vent conversation.

He was at the third stage. His temperament was far more poised than I believe mine would have been. His liver was terribly bad, we used to have to call man-down so the CLOs could come and escort him to the prison infirmary for medical treatment.

It wasn't much they could do for his fatal condition, but to inject Novocain into him to relieve his excruciating pain in his liver. I surmise that he'll get better.

But I don't have his current condition, for it has been more than a year since we departed. I hope that somehow he is restored back to health that would allow him to live many more years.

Speedy owned a very large medical encyclopedia that contained every disease known to the science of man. I asked him if I could use it, being curious about my fading skin condition. I perused through it as I researched my skin condition and I was able to diagnose my condition. The book guided me to all of the symptoms that I was experiencing. This skin disease is called Vitiligo, a skin (disease) disorder characterized by patches of white skin due to loss of pigment cells (melanocytes). It's not contagious or lethal, thank God for that, because this condition is beyond me bringing it upon myself.

Any part of the body may be affected. Common sites of pigment loss are around the eyes, nose, and mouth; on the hands and genitals; and at sites of injury.

I have it around my nose, under my lower lip where you first noticed the very small spot, and my fingers, and toes, and the peripheral of my hands and feet, and very small spots that's hardly noticeable on various parts of my person.

According to the book, stress brings rapid advancement to the disease. God knows these wicked Institutional Gang Investigating (IGI) officials here in Pelican Bay SHU aren't helping my condition in relieving stress. In fact, they have brought more stress to me in one year than I have experienced in the duration of my thirty years of imprisonment.

A couple of months after I diagnosed myself with my skin condition, I went to another block to cell up with my homie (friend) name Mad Moe again, for the third time within the five dramatic years since we have met.

I asked him did he notice my fading coloration. He said, "Yeah, a little, (after a close examination) but it's not like damn, look at dude. We (homies) are gonna love you if you turned all white," he said with a light sincere smile that indicated my stature within the prison system amongst our tribe is unprecedented.

And it is guys like him, Mom, who is considered gang members that I feel more love for than my own so-called biological family.

There is not a medical explanation to how this disease is obtained. There is no cure, but treatment to some degree.

The irony about this condition is many of years ago when Michael Jackson was being interviewed by Oprah Winfrey, she asked him about his skin turning white. I used to despise him severely. I thought it was disgusting that a person could alter their physical appearance to simulate what they are not.

When he declared his diagnosis I didn't believe any such disease existed. But boy, was I wrong for judging his condition, which I can say has imbued me with the principles of not judging people without the true facts.

I love you Mom, indelibly,
Your son, free Mike

Loving Thy Enemies

Dear Mom,

First and foremost I trust and pray that you are well. I am doing alright myself considering the inhumane conditions that we are subject to here in the Pelican Bay SHU.

Mom I sincerely understand what you are telling me about the Bible's teaching of loving thy enemies and being kind to those who are unkind to me—for God will see me through.

I know that you mean well, Mom, and want to see me free of harm and depression. But it's hard to love people who treat you like animals merely because of their sadistically desire to oppress you for being a black man.

I know that you are going to disagree with my belief, for you are profoundly devoted to the teaching of the Bible. But I believe the Bible has indoctrinated black people to be passively submissive to thralldom while the oppressors tread down on us at will.

All black elderly mothers teach their children to be sullen in the faces of authority for fear of being slain by the evil of the races system.

And what baffles me is that our mothers and fathers cry for our need to be passive is not based upon theory of non-violence. Because y'all beat us so severely that it could be tantamount to what the 1800's slaves had to endure by their wicked slave masters. I wholeheartedly believe that the black folks indoctrinated this scourging stigma as a curse from slavery. And it became our own worst enemy and it is why the urban youths believe that violence is the panacea to solving all problems. I recall as a lad when you whipped me as harsh as the police or rival gangs.

And the most agonizing part about that was I dared not to fight you back, just accepted the ravaging punishment like a good ole slave child.

Which ultimately made me more viciously inclined to deal with my problems in such a savage way when people violated my space. I now believe that putting ones hands on my person in an inappropriate manner is not justifiable. You cannot beat principles or correct behavior into people—or into all people.

I'll tell you, Mom, if whippings were the source of solution in my life, I would have been one of the nation's finest citizens. But look at me, one of the nation's most troubled –by the standard of mainstream America.

A couple of years ago, Mom, I told you I was back in Pelican Bay SHU for an assault on aCorrectional Officer (CO).

Well I really tried to do everything possible to do right by prison rules when I was in general population. I stayed out there for five months.

One day while I was on the yard occupied with about two hundred prisoners, a CO and I engaged in a heated dispute. He became so irate that he stormed into my face and commenced to poking me in my chest with an angry force. I tried with all my might to suppress my distraught reaction.

But after the 6th poke I could no longer maintain my composure, which led me to swinging at him. Had he done his job in a professional manner I would have complied to the rules. There are so many cowards in these prisons that the COs feel that they can treat everyone like they are less than human. Many of these officials don't adhere to the law or prison rules when it is not to their advantage.

I did two years for the confrontation with the CO and after that they (prison administration) had to figure out a way to keep me out of the general population. So the Institutional Gang Investigating Unit (IGI) falsely concocted prison documents claiming that I am an associate to a particular prison gang that I have despised all of my prison life.

This was the only way that they could legally keep me off of their General Population (GP) for such a long time. It's a six year Security Housing Unit term that can easily be reacted into more years by the simple words of malfeasant COs or prison informers. Then they confiscated my manuscript, saying it was a danger to the safety and security of the prison. When in fact, the Tehachapi prison IGI officials seized this same manuscript. They vetted it thoroughly and returned it to me with some inspiring words that the book was good and it have the potentials to help trouble youths.

By which they granted me the liberty to send you the manuscript on several occurrences while I was in their jurisdiction (prison). Hence, it would be illogically unfair for me to consider all of these white prison officials to be prejudice or incompetent of making objective decisions when it's relating to their personal prejudice. Some are decent officials.

But I knew that sooner or later I was going to have some unpleasant encounter with officials who are motivated by hatred, which I believe was the case with the Pelican Bay officials.

As you know Mom, I filled a "writ for habeas corpus" (law suit) against the prison for seizing my manuscripts. It was a good thing that you made a copy of the original manuscript when Tehachapi granted me the opportunity to send it home.

Because it's not easy an easy way up here in the hills of Crescent City, California dealing with the judicial system. To a black or brown man, our justice is decided upon by the decisions of a kangaroo court.

Dealing with the legal system as such, is like me telling the Grand Wizard of the KKK, a young skinhead called me a nigger. The racist system just doesn't work for us, is why we are the predominate race throughout the nation's prison system. It is not that we are the vilest people by nature, that is what the stealthy foes of the urban communities would love to have people to believe.

The judiciary, law enforcement, and other social powers are and were designed to keep us ignorant to our own self-destruction. And I reiterate, the destructive lifestyle that we live is their livelihood.

Imagine if the urban communities suddenly became crime free. That would place millions of suburban and thousands of urban people under unemployment.

So you see how important it is for certain government officials to not abolish crime completely.

They only want to maintain it under their control, to the point where it's not too much or too little.

The Judge of Del Norte Superior Court denied my writ for habeas corpus against the prison, this surprised me to a slight degree.

Because I know that when I set out to compose the book it was delineated to condemn gang violence and illicit behavior—with hopes that the disseminating message would galvanize some of the guys in society and prison to help correct our nefarious conditions. Because if we don't correct it, it will perpetuate for only God knows how long.

I mean, Mom, an autobiography is when one writes about his own life. How could I write a book, a peaceful lifestyle with my history? It wouldn't be a truthful depiction of my life. And had I not been through what I had, the guys who need to be reached wouldn't give my words an inkling of a thought. Many of them can relate to my experiences as I can to theirs.

I had always admired the persona of the TV Judge, Judge Mathis, but now I had the opportunity to hear him on BET "106 & Park" (musical video show) sharing his personal opinions and deeds of helping correct the urban blight.

I respect him immensely. I can almost guarantee that if lofty officials such as Judge Mathis and Attorney General Eric Holder read the book and judged merits of it they would support the message, of course condemn the negative activity as I do too when I reflect back on my early years. For I no longer align myself with criminal activities.

The Attorney General and Judge genuinely care about the urban blight and understand its dialect and way of life. When Mr. Eric Holder uttered those blazoning words to the nation, "We are a nation of cowards!" I was dumb-founded to the blatant truth that he declared to the nation. Speaking about the diabolical deeds of racism that is keeping this country from reaching its fullest potential. From the subordinate and lofty officials to the common people who are afraid to speak against the misdeed of others for fear of pariah reprisal from colleague, friends, and family.

Lofty officials such as the Attorney General and Judge are inside officials of the judicial branch of the government and are very cognizant to the Machiavellian functioning of those officials who are possessed by the evil will to tread down urban youths, who don't stand a chance against such horrendous force. Who have created this vile condition that exists within our communities that are so looked down upon.

When those such as myself reform ourselves and become an impulsive force of change for the betterment of our conditions, they (officials) quarantine us from the masses of young and old brothers who are benighted so we won't be able to imbue them with the knowledge and principles needed to begin to rectify our conditions.

So Mom, it's difficult for me to say or believe that I don't hate my adversaries who hate me abysmally just because God made me a darker color. I will have to pray and ask God to render me the strength to forgive my enemies who treats me like dreg. But I can honestly delineate that I don't hate people based upon race, or lifestyle they live as long as it's not harming other people.

My greatest hero was a white man. The 1800's abolitionist John Brown, who I think was the greatest man who ever trod upon earth.

You see Mom, the reason I place him above our black liberators is because they were also fighting for their own liberty. Because of that, it was a natural impulse for them to join the struggle.

But John Brown had his human rights, he could have very well succumbed to the evil practice of the mainstream society of the 1800's. they declared that John Brown was mentally ill because he vigorously lived for abolishing slavery. But today it is clear that those who embraced this wicked system were socially ill and a moral hazard to humanity and John Brown was the one of proper sanity.

Mom, a few months ago you sent me a letter and made a comment, "Thank God for Obama." I never responded to the comment because at this point my opinion is low. I have never heard him say anything concerning he's fighting for the urban communities. It's always he's fighting for the middle class. Middle class already have ninety percent of the congress fighting for them. I recall looking at a presidential news conference and Andra Showell, a BET news correspondent asked Obama what he was going to do for the job shortages in the urban communities, and I noticed that Obama was kind of in a snit about that question. But he replied that he's working to restore the middle class recessions because when the middle class is doing well we all are. I disagree.

You are the only person in society, who I received a letter from who spoke laudable in this name, in fact, who even mentioned his name. I like his temperament as a person as far as what I see on television. But I'll hold on to my opinion to what Denzel Washington stated on TV when he was asked his opinion about Obama. "Let's wait and see what he does," he said. So that's the stand that I'm taking.

Denzel has proven his authenticity to the community, so I'm following his wisdom.

As Black people we are always extolling people who have yet to prove themselves as spearheads of our communities. President Jimmy Carter was more of a black president to me than Obama. Still to this day he stand firm on shining the light on racism that Obama be trying to shun. I was supporting Hillary Clinton to the fullest because she was a proponent for black people before Obama emerged upon the political scene. And those black folks who voted for Obama simply because he's black, that's the trait of Black racism.

Having said that about the President, for the good of Attorney General Eric Holder and the First Lady Mitchell Obama, we need to support the President for a second term to keep them in the position of influence.

They represent all of the people in the nation in a fair and dignified way. I do not dislike President Obama, I just get tired of hearing him put emphasis on how he's indicating to urban Americans,

"To hell with y'all!" That's the way I interpret his declaration in his speeches. And another thing I dislike is when the President praise his idol, the sixteenth president of the United States, Abraham Lincoln, who freed the slaves, which President Obama proudly declared. But you misguide the people and its true history when you don't reveal the facts. Yes, Abraham Lincoln freed us from bondage. But it wasn't inspired from the goodness of his heart for human rights, like John Brown, it was inspired by economical advantage for the country. I believe that people need to know these kinds of things of our history.

Well Mom, I am coming upon my thirty-one years of incarceration. I recall in 2003 when I resided in Tehachapi State Prison you and Dorine came to visit me. I can vividly recall you telling me you didn't know me anymore since I have been away for so long.

As for my likes and dislikes. Well Mom, I hope that in this lengthy epistle it will summarize my mental growth and principles by which I have philosophized in this point of my life. I can genuinely declare that I possess no deprecation about my life's circumstances because I know that there are millions of people in society and prison whose situations are much more inconsolable than mines.

And I actually feel compassion for them when I see children and innocent people suffering on TV.

But when I feel stressful at times in dealing with my unpleasant condition, I think about the victim to whom I am convicted of. And for certain I would render my life to resurrect his if it were earthly possible. Though I was a young grotesque, wayward fool and a victim of my circumstances in an urban society created for young people such as myself to succumb to failure.

I love you ineffably,
Mike

A book so dangerous that it was filed "Under Seal" in court proceeding to determine if it should ever see the light of day.

The above phrase is my paraphrase to the biased theory of the Pelican Bay State Prison Security Housing Unit I.G.I. officials and the Judge who supported their canarded decision.

The Judge didn't have the decency of equity to read the entire manuscript to determine the value of the literature as a whole. Before rendering his decision, in which my counsel strongly suggested. It is not by chance that the black and brown urban people flood these prison yards. In part of the Judge's decision he stated that he read portions of the book that my counsel and I submitted as well as the Respondent (DA) as evidence. Then he went on later to say that the whole book was violent without meaningful solution. When, in fact, he didn't even read the entire book. When we are subject to this type of injustice, people always wonder why urban youths and people of our communities (across the nation) have such a disdainful attitude towards the judicial system and its law enforcement.

My solution to this inequity is for gang dudes to start destroying this mentality that we have in taking pride in having our children, lil' brothers, sisters, and other young family members joining our gangs. And start imbuing them with the mettle of it's cool to be judges. DAs, COs and the many other legal professions needed to rectify this unfair system in which we dwell.

Final Comment

I once saw a TV show on BET featuring the lil' rapper T.I. I was surprised to hear him blurt "Prison is for losers." But yet he keeps coming back for trivial cases.

Perhaps, if you stop going to them prison camps and come around brothers of my stature, whose recalcitrant to oppression and fully conscious to why we are so-called "losers," you might learn something.

If you're not aware of the fact that we are an oppress people in this country, you shouldn't speak on our affairs.

This system was designed to make people like you and me losers. Even though some people of our community succeed, it may give mirage that we have overcame, but the reality is we are still living by the hateful doctrine of Willie Lynch, the 1700's slave breaker. The disturbingly sick thing about it is we are constantly contributing to our own thralldom.

Willie Lynch instilled into us (slaves) to hate one another by pitching old black males against the young black mates, the young black males against the old black males, the light-skinned blacks against the dark-skinned blacks, the dark-skinned blacks against the light-skinned blacks.

These mentioned infusions are just two of the diabolical weapons they utilized to keep a people enslaved and ignorant. He instilled into slave owners to trust no black.

When we succumb to disseminating division amongst ourselves by pitching ourselves against one Another, we are proponent of the Willie Lynch doctrine that has been very apocalyptic and detrimental to our community and the growth as a people because the vast majority of us are still poor and oppress.

I heard the young dude Terrence on the show "106 & Park" speak very pejorative to the massive of young urban brothers who probably value his (Terrence) life as they would smash an insect. He called them cowards and made a clear declaration that he would snitch on them, that kind of hostility and hatred is not being part of the solution, it only serves to exacerbate hatred.

In the struggle against racism in Martin Luther King era, he taught us that love and respect was the most powerful weapon against your foes. So why don't you dudes who are TV personalities use the King's doctrine to reach your own young troubled people. It would be more beneficial and I believe they would listen if they respect you. I use to speak highly of Terrence to them, seeing a young brother doing his thing on TV, up until he starts speaking tactless. You dudes need to leave the social dialogue to community activist like Jeff Johnson who has social skills and veracity that we all respect.

I suggest that you brothers check your mouth piece, the language that you utilize is promoting utter disrespect to the legion of Damus and Kiwes nationwide, who are noble, race conscious, and determine to elevate despite our incubus condition or surroundings.

A loser is one who has no sense of desire to achieve goals in their life and content with vagabondage, regardless of their placement, may it be behind prison walls or in society. So young brothers, be sagacious to what you expect or ate out of your mouth, we are listening.

In chapter five of this memoir, I made a comment that I "truly" wish to recant. I said "Pelican Bay SHU was the best thing to happen to me." Though the inhumane solitary conditions stem violent behavior, it is like a sullen incendiary just waiting to fulminate the first time that someone enrage you, at least for me.

You cannot isolate a human being indefinitely or for a long period of time (without appropriate human relations with others) and then relinquish them and expect them to have a normal state of being.

By means of hunger strikes (statewide in the California State Prison System) there has been international attention brought to the writhing conditions of Pelican Bay State Prison Security Housing Unit.

Hence, the appropriate authorities vowed to ameliorate the harsh conditions. Thus far, there have been steps taken to rectify these inhumane conditions.

Upon the completion of this memoir, my life in prison spiraled into a contingent trajectory of Continuance Drama. To which I have recently composed two other books, titled "Continuance Drama" and "Anecdotes by the Most Infamous." Both of them, I assure you, are humdingers. See contents on the following pages.

"CONTINUANCE DRAMA"

CONTENTS

Part-1:   The Investigation ....

Part-2:   No, Pelican Bay Welcome Madame ....

Part-3:   Roc' and Hotdog..

Part-4:   Crip, Crip, Crip, Crip, Muthaf—ka, Crip..........................

Part-5:   Bad to the Bone ....

Part-6:   Behavior Modification Unit (BMU ....

Part-7:   BMU Graduation..

Part-8:   The Plot..

Part-9:   A Very Irate CO ....

Part-10: Back to the Pelican Bay SHU ....

Part-11: Misogyny is not my Intention ....

SUPPLEMENT

A Message to Oprah Winfrey and Bill Cosby.......................

"ANECDOTES by the MOST INFAMOUS"

CONTENTS

Section-1:   Trying to Bully a Ridah (warrior.....................................

Section-2:   Big Talk and No Action ....

Section-3:   Damn, Ms. Lovelace...

Section-4:   The Hardest Young Homie on the Yard ....

Section-5:   Scandalous Gambling..

Section-6:   Holy Letters from Pookie and my Mom ....

Section-7:   "Tweet me, I'll Snitch on Them", he exclaimed..............

Section-8:   Police Values..

Section-9:   I Wept (The Jane Pittman Story ....

Section:10:   A Plea for the Development of Wise,

                Committed, and Race Conscious

Bloods and Crips (Damus/Kiwes) ....

CPSIA information can be obtained at www.ICGtesting.com
Printed in the USA
LVOW12*1916091213

364554LV00012B/620/P